PRAYER COUNTRY

PRAYER COUNTRY
A TOUR GUIDE TO THE WONDERS OF PRAYER

DOROTHY EATON WATTS

Pacific Press Publishing Association
Boise, Idaho
Oshawa, Ontario, Canada

Edited by Jerry D. Thomas
Designed by Tim Larson
Cover photo by Shoji Yoshida / Image Bank ®
Typeset in 10/12 New Century Schoolbook

Library of Congress Cataloging-in-Publication Data:

Watts, Dorothy Eaton, 1937-
    Prayer country: a tour guide to the wonders of prayer /
Dorothy Eaton Watts.
      p. cm.
    ISBN 0-8163-1112-9
    1. Prayer. 2. Watts, Dorothy Eaton, 1937-   . I. Title.
BV215.W37   1993
248.3'2—dc20   92-14847
                                            CIP

96 97 ● 5

Contents

Welcome to Prayer Country

Come with me on a journey, on several journeys, into the land and experience of prayer.

This book was written with you in mind. I know you have needs and problems for which prayer is the only answer. I know, because I, too, have those needs. We all do. We all need regular trips to Prayer Country because we all need a real, talking relationship with our heavenly Father.

Much of this book is a record of my own experiences with prayer. On too many of my journeys into Prayer Country, I was what you might call a "shopper." I crossed the border knowing exactly what I wanted to find. As each souvenir was located, I ticked it off my list.

My keys were lost. I prayed and immediately thought of a place to look. There they were! A small miracle. A souvenir of Prayer Country. Check. Prayer answered.

All my friends in academy had skates. I wanted some too, but I didn't have the money. I prayed, and a few days later a letter from a family friend arrived with money in it, just enough for a pair of skates. Another miracle. A souvenir on my list. Check. Prayer answered.

My first piano recital was coming up. During an afternoon practice, I was so nervous that my fingers stumbled over the keyboard and my knees literally shook. I went to my room and claimed the promise, "I can do all things through Christ which strengtheneth me." I played my recital piece that night flawlessly and with confidence. A miracle for sure. Check. Prayer answered.

I wanted to marry a minister. I prayed about it, and God worked a few miracles in bringing Ron into my life. Another souvenir to check off. Prayer answered.

I wanted a baby, but after four years of trying, I wasn't pregnant. No problem. I'd just make sure God saw that it was on my shopping list as I entered Prayer Country. I put "baby" on top of the list and circled it to make sure there was no mistake. I visited doctors, certain that the miracle would occur. It didn't. More years went by, but miracle babies were in short supply. There were none for me.

"Why, God, why?" I cried out in my pain. "I thought You could do anything, even give children to barren women. You did it for Sarah and Hannah; why not for me?" Tears. Disappointment. "God, don't You see how much I want this souvenir!" Silence.

We went to India as missionaries. One day as I drove on a crowded street, a man suddenly stepped in front of my scooter. I pressed hard on the brakes, but not soon enough. I hit him head on. He lay unconscious in the hospital for eight days. I practically lived in Prayer Country that week. There was only one item on my shopping list. Let that man live!

"Please, God, please! Forget the baby, forget everything else I ever asked for; give me this one miracle, the life of this man!" He died. Miracles were out of stock. Prayer didn't seem to work, so I stopped praying.

For two years I stayed outside the borders of the Great Land of Prayer. No one else knew my struggle. I knelt beside my bed at night so that Ron would think I was praying as usual, but inside I shook my fist at God and said, "I'm angry with You, God. You can do anything, yet You refused to do this one small favor for me. You can keep Your souvenirs. You can keep Your miracles! I don't want to visit You anymore! It doesn't do any good!"

So I stayed away from Prayer Country. Now and again I met enthusiastic Christians, thrilled with their prayer experiences, waving their miracles for the world to see. "Look at my souvenir!" they testified. "See what God has done for me!"

At first, when I heard these people speak, it made me angry.

Why them? Why not me? Then, by and by, I stopped feeling angry and felt instead a wistful longing for Prayer Country. How nice it had been in those days when I'd traveled with the King.

About this time a beggar came to our gate, and I turned her away with unkind words, with no hint of mercy or love.

"Dorothy, Dorothy," Ron said to me. "What has happened to you? What's wrong?"

"Nothing," I said as I turned away, but down deep I knew the source of the trouble.

"The darkness of the evil one encloses those who neglect to pray," says Ellen White. I was feeling that darkness, that emptiness which comes to a soul without God. I had no light, no love, no joy to share.

I needed a trip to Prayer Country; I needed to meet the King once more. Only this time I went without a shopping list, and what a difference it has made!

Types of travelers

Among Christians, there are two different types of people who pray: those who are looking for answers and those who are looking for God. Or, you might say, there are two basic types of travelers who visit Prayer Country: the Shoppers and the Hunters.

Shoppers come to Prayer Country looking for miracles; they want God to give healing, provide money, supply strength, or fix a broken relationship. Shoppers take seriously the promises that say, "With God all things are possible," and "My God shall supply all your need," and come looking for a way out of difficulty.

Shoppers come to Prayer Country to get something from God. They spend their journey looking for spiritual slot machines where they can pull the handles and get a miracle. They think if they say the right words, live the right life, or push the right buttons with God, He'll give them what they want, a miracle of answered prayer.

Shoppers tend to look at the souvenirs of answered prayers other travelers have collected, and they feel a little bit jealous if it doesn't happen that way with them. When Shoppers don't get everything on their shopping list, they leave feeling cheated.

They didn't find what they were looking for, and many decide that a journey into Prayer Country doesn't live up to the advertising blurbs. They asked for a miracle, and miracles seemed to be out of stock. It didn't work, so why keep trying?

Hunters, on the other hand, go into Prayer Country with an entirely different motive. Their purpose is to meet the King of Prayer Country. While they believe in miracles, and often collect them along their journey, those are incidental to the main reason for their trip.

Hunters are looking for a deeper prayer experience, a closer relationship with God, a real mountaintop spiritual experience. They are not looking for answers; they are looking for God.

Oswald Chambers was a Hunter. In his book, *My Utmost for His Highest*, he says, "Whenever the insistence is on the point that God answers prayer, we are off the track. The meaning of prayer is that we get hold of God, not of the answer" (p. 27).

In *The Answer Is Prayer*, Morris Venden states that "the primary purpose in prayer is communion with God" (p. 37). In this he agrees with Ellen White, who said, "Prayer is the opening of the heart to God as to a friend. Not that it is necessary in order to make known to God what we are, but in order to enable us to receive Him. Prayer does not bring God down to us, but brings us up to Him" (*Steps to Christ,* p. 93).

The whole meaning of a journey into Prayer Country is to find God, not answers. For once we have found God, the answers don't matter. Whether He says Yes, No, or Wait a while is unimportant, because we have found Him. We know we can trust the King of Prayer Country to choose our souvenirs.

This book will share some of my experiences in my search for the King of Prayer Country and some of the paths I have found that have led me to a stronger, more consistent prayer life.

Yes, I still have a list of needs as I pray. But it's an agenda of needs that I discuss with God rather than an order to be filled, down to the color and catalog number. As the King of Prayer Country, God has the right to cross needs off my list and add other items to it. As long as I walk with Him, it doesn't really matter what God does with my requests, for I know I can trust Him to do what is best.

The eleven tours outlined in this book are not, then, sure ways to gather miracles. Rather, they are routes that other travelers have discovered which can lead to a deeper relationship with the King of Prayer Country. If you choose, this book can be used as a practical guide to strengthen your prayer life.

How to use this as a guidebook

1. Read through the guidebook once to get a picture of the various routes.

2. Choose one of the tours. Read that chapter again.

3. Follow the directions under "Experience the Tour."

4. Try that prayer pattern for several days before choosing another route to explore.

5. If you desire more information on this particular tour, check in the chapter notes at the end of this book for a bibliography of available material.

TOUR ONE

The Palms Route

Are you OK?" Nita asked as she passed me in the church foyer. "You look tired."

"Oh?" I replied, straightening my shoulders and smiling. "I had a busy week, but I'll survive."

Actually, I hadn't slept well for over two months. My shoulder, stiffly frozen for unknown reasons, filled my days and nights with pain. Daily physical therapy was using up every ounce of energy I had. There was little left for my part-time job or the freelance writing assignments that were piling up undone. Several speaking appointments were hanging over my head as well as a women's retreat for which I was responsible.

At the door of the sanctuary, I struggled to gain my composure before entering. I frowned and breathed deeply as pain shot down my right arm. One of the elders came to my side and whispered, "Smile! You look upset."

"Sorry," I answered, with my best smile.

I spotted an empty seat beside my friend, Deb. I sat down beside her and willed my body to relax as I listened to the soft organ music. It wasn't working.

Deb leaned over and said, "You look sad. I don't know what's wrong, but I want you to know someone is thinking nice thoughts about you."

"Thanks," I replied, again trying hard to smile and look relaxed.

I prayed all through the service, but the tension was still there as I walked out the church doors. Each day I prayed for strength and release from pain, but there was no relief.

Later that week, I started reading *Celebration of Discipline,* by Richard J. Foster. On page 31, he suggests a prayer route I had never tried, a method he calls "Palms Down, Palms Up." It involves using your hands to symbolize releasing your burdens to God. Relieved to find that it had nothing to do with New Age religions or meditation, I was willing to try it.

I stopped reading and picked up my journal. Turning to a blank page, I wrote out a "Palms Down, Palms Up" prayer. Leaning back in my chair, I placed my hands in a palms-down position along my legs, indicating my desire to turn over all my concerns to God. I kept my hands in that position as I prayed my "Palms Down" prayer.

Palms Down

"Lord, I give You my pain and my frustration about the slowness of healing." I paused, pushing my hands down and away from my body as though actually throwing the frustration on the floor at Jesus' feet.

"Lord, I want You to take my writing too. Take my tensions and guilt for not doing more, my inability just now to be creative, to focus and accomplish. Take all my feelings of being at a dead end in my career. I can't deal with this; it's Yours!"

I could almost feel the tensions dropping away. My burden was growing lighter.

"There's more, Lord," I continued. "I surrender the women's retreat all to You. I feel such a burden to get seminar leaders. I don't know who to have or where to find them. Take this burden, please. And then there's my schedule. I know it's my fault for planning too much. I want You to take my anxiety and frustration about trying to do it all. Please take the stress from me—I don't want it. Take it all. The whole schedule is Yours. Change it or do whatever You want with it. I can't cope with it."

This was fun! I was actually smiling at the thought of the big pile of frustrations I had just handed over to the Lord!

Palms Up

Next, I placed my hands in a palms-up position, symbolic of

my desire to receive something from the Lord, and began again to pray aloud.

"Lord, I'd like to receive Your healing power in my arm. And further, I'd like to receive Your patience to endure however long that takes.

"Lord, then, about my writing," I continued. "I'd like Your guidance and some encouragement. I'll need a new sense of joy, fulfillment, energy, and inspiration if You'd have me continue."

I sat with my palms open in a receiving position, waiting, listening. In the silence, God spoke to my heart, and I understood Him to say, "You need to rest for a few months. I'll let you know when it's time to write again."

"About the retreat, Lord," I pressed on. "I want to receive strength and wisdom, but I need more than that. I want You to give me six seminar leaders by next Sunday.

"And I want to receive Your peace in the midst of my too-full schedule, and Your power, love, and strength to do what must get done."

I sat for a while in silence, my palms still open, ready to receive whatever the Lord had to give. I could feel God's presence very near, His love, peace, and joy warming my whole body. There was something about the physical involvement with my hands that made that morning's prayer experience very meaningful.

As I have reflected on why the Palms Down, Palms Up prayer is such an effective one, I have decided it is because it so plainly is a prayer of surrender, of releasing everything into God's hands. It is an acting out of Peter's suggestion in 1 Peter 5:7, "Casting all of your care upon him; for he careth for you." "You can throw the whole weight of your anxieties upon him, for you are his personal concern," says Phillips, revised edition. The International Children's Bible puts it even more simply, "Give all your worries to him, because he cares for you."

> Take to Him everything that perplexes the mind. Nothing is too great for Him to bear, for He holds up worlds, He rules over all the affairs of the universe. Nothing that in any way concerns our peace is too small for Him to notice. There is no chapter in our experience

too dark for Him to read; there is no perplexity too difficult for Him to unravel. No calamity can befall the least of His children, no anxiety harass the soul, no joy cheer, no sincere prayer escape the lips, of which our heavenly Father is unobservant, or in which He takes no immediate interest. . . . The relations between God and each soul are as distinct and full as though there were not another soul upon the earth to share His watchcare, not another soul for whom He gave His beloved Son (*Steps to Christ*, p. 100).

Foster suggests that after the praying is finished, you sit for several moments in complete silence. He says, "Do not ask for anything. Allow the Lord to commune with you, to love you. If impressions or directions come, fine; if not, fine."

I've found as I have traveled the Palms Route on several occasions, that God often does speak in the silence, bringing to mind a verse of Scripture or perhaps a reminder of something I should do or something I need to leave undone.

In that silent, waiting time, God seems very close. Priorities suddenly begin to emerge, and life feels ordered again.

God responds

The next day I wrote in my journal, "I feel much more at peace about the retreat and the myriad other things I have in my schedule. My spirit is lifting. You have already begun to answer yesterday's prayer! Thank You, Lord!"

That was Thursday. By Sunday I had not only the six seminar speakers I had requested, but a seventh as well! God had proved again that He is able to do "abundantly above all that we ask or think."

The arm pain gradually began to improve. On Sabbath, July 7, while at the General Conference session in Indianapolis, I was dressing and suddenly realized that for the first time I was putting my arm over my head without pain. Today, I have full use of the arm, even though the doctor had predicted that it would never return to its normal range of use.

About two weeks later, on July 23, I was reading in John 5

about the healing of the lame man by the pool of Bethesda. Verse 8 seemed to stand out on the page as God's special message for me. I wrote in my journal, "Lord, I seem to hear You saying to me, 'Rise, Dorothy, take up your pen and write.' After seven months of deadness, withered creativity, and inability to concentrate on writing, a time of rest and reflection on my priorities, at last the time has come to take up my pen and write."

A deeper relationship

The next few paragraphs in my journal indicate how the Palms Route had done much more than produce souvenirs of answered prayer; it had led me into a deeper relationship with Jesus.

"Lord, help me to get my priorities straight each day, to take time for You, for Ron, for myself, so that I don't again get into the state I was in last winter. Teach me to consider, to take time to think things through, and to say No when necessary. Help me to say No to the good so that I might say Yes to the best.

"Life is too short to waste. Help me, Lord, to take time to see the flowers, hear the birds, revel in Your marvelous world of beauty, to enjoy the simple things of life at home.

"I read something really good from Oswald Chambers this morning: 'Faith never knows where it is being led, but it loves and knows the one who is leading.'

"Lord, I confess my sin of wanting to know where You are leading, of trying to discern Your purpose for my life, when I should better have used my energy to love and know You, the One who is leading!

"Lord, I do love You, and where You lead does not really matter! The important thing is walking with You, not where we walk."

Experience the tour

1. Fold a sheet of blank paper lengthwise, dividing the sheet into two vertical columns.

2. Write "Palms Down" at the top of the left-hand column. Under that column identify each worry you want to give away to God. Write out a sentence or two about each concern, telling

God you want Him to take it from you.

3. Write "Palms Up" at the top of the right-hand column. Under that column, opposite each concern, write what you would like to receive from God to take its place.

4. Take a position in which you are comfortable in talking to God. You can sit in your favorite chair, with your hands resting on your lap, or kneel in a quiet spot, with your hands on your bed or a chair.

5. Pray your prayer aloud to God, first the "Palms Down" column, then the "Palms Up" column.

6. Sit for a while in complete silence. Allow God to speak to you if He so chooses, bringing to your mind texts, the words of a song, or something He wants you to do.

7. Make a written note of any impressions that come to you during this quiet time of listening and waiting before Him. You may want to use a different-colored pen or pencil to write in notes beside each concern as you see God working on your behalf.

8. Lay one hand on a sheet of paper. Trace around your thumb and fingers. Cut out the drawing you have made. On one side write a Palms Down prayer. Turn it over and write your Palms Up petition. Place it in your Bible. Pray your Palms Down, Palms Up prayer daily until the answer comes.

9. Use your hands during the day in quick prayers for help in situations that arise. Place your palms down for a brief moment as you silently pray, "Lord, take this feeling [anger, frustration, worry, fear, jealousy, etc.] from me." Then quickly turn your hands up, again praying silently, "In its place, Lord, please give me Your [peace, love, understanding, trust, calmness, etc.]."

10. Try a Palms Down, Palms Up prayer when you can't sleep at night. Let your arms go limp on the mattress in a palms-down position. Try to imagine Jesus reaching down to take each burden as you hand it over to Him. Then turn your palms up and imagine Him putting blessings of peace, trust, and quiet sleep into your open palms.

TOUR TWO

The Eggs Expedition

D o you have a baby nobody wants?" I asked the chief medical officer of a government hospital in Bangalore, India. "I know a couple in the United States who want to adopt a baby girl."

"As a matter of fact, we do have." The doctor nodded. "The baby was brought in last night, found along the roadside in a garbage bin, I believe."

"Is it a police case?" I asked.

"No, we haven't yet reported the incident to the police. You can take the baby with no trouble at all."

This was good news! Already I had spent several days trying to get two baby girls released from another hospital. It was a long procedure because it involved taking the case to court and persuading a judge to release the children.

"Where is the baby?" I asked eagerly.

The doctor flipped through some charts and studied them for a moment before replying, "Maternity ward, block A. It's the new block of buildings on the other side of the main entrance. You'll have no trouble finding it. Just ask the sister in charge for the baby brought in last night."

I found the maternity ward without difficulty. A gray-haired, matronly nurse frowned as I walked in.

"Yes?" she questioned, but her look said much more. It was as though she were saying, "What business do you have here? Can't you see how busy we are?"

"The baby," I said nervously. "The one brought in last night.

The one found by the roadside. I came to see it."

"No baby came in last night," she said.

"But the medical officer told me to come here to find it," I insisted. "Don't you have an abandoned baby here somewhere?"

"No! We have no abandoned baby here. The medical officer must have made a mistake. Now, if you'll excuse me." She turned and walked away.

I walked along a shaded veranda to the next block. Again the answer was the same, "No baby here." The hospital was a huge, sprawling complex, started during the days of British occupation and added to, haphazardly, through the years. I wandered in and out of buildings and up and down stairs, peeking into wards, not at all sure of where I was going, but not wanting to give up my search for the baby.

At last, I walked up some stairs and came to a long, open room that had rows of cots down each side. Children of all ages lay or sat on the beds. Beside many of the beds was a mother or a grandmother talking softly to the child. From the other end of the room, a nurse replaced a bedside chart and walked toward me.

"Were you looking for someone?" she asked.

"Yes, an abandoned baby who was brought in last night," I said. "The medical officer said I could take the baby, but I can't find it. Is it here?"

"None came in last night," she said. "But we do have a baby girl brought in five weeks ago. She was left on the hospital steps in a bundle of rags. Why don't you take her?"

She turned then and led me to a nearby crib. The first thing I noticed was the bottle of intravenous fluid hanging on a stand to the right of the crib, its tube leading to her arm. Scabbed-over sores covered her face, neck, and bony arms. Her eyes were open, staring at the ceiling. I spoke to her, but she made no movement. I moved my hands in front of her eyes, but she did not respond.

"She has diarrhea," explained the nurse. "We've had to feed her intravenously ever since she came in. She won't suck." With that, the nurse picked up a full bottle from the windowsill. She put the nipple in the baby's mouth and propped up the bottle with a pillow.

"See. She won't suck," the nurse declared.

"But why don't you hold her and try to feed her?" I asked. "Babies need touching; they need lots of love."

"Lady." The nurse sighed and shook her head. "We have fifty beds in this ward, and there are only two of us to look after all these children. We have no time for holding babies!"

Tears filled my eyes as I looked at the frail little girl lying so still in the crib. "I have a mother for you," I told her. "Someone to hold you and love you. I'll come back and get you soon."

I ran down the steps and across the lawn to the office of the chief medical officer. He looked up from his desk as I stood in the door to catch my breath.

"I couldn't find the baby you told me about," I blurted out, "but there is a little girl up in the children's ward in the old building." I pointed to a building just inside the gate of the hospital compound. "She's been there for five weeks. I want to take her home."

The doctor studied his charts for what seemed like forever; then he replied, "Sorry. We have no abandoned girl in that ward. None at all."

"But I saw her with my own eyes!" I exclaimed. "She's there and she's so sick. She needs someone to love her. Please, sir, call the nurse on that ward. That child is there."

He nodded, picked up the receiver, and dialed. "Do you have an abandoned girl in your ward?" he asked. "Hmmm! I see. It's OK. You can give her to the American lady. No problem."

"Amazing!" he said as he hung up. "She's not in our records. You may take her home."

"Now?"

"Sure. Why not?"

Why not? I thought. Because I'm not ready to take a baby home. I came on a motor scooter. I have no diapers, no baby formula, no bottles, no crib, no blankets. I don't even know how to take care of a baby, since we adopted our three as older children.

I brushed aside my doubts and said, "Thank you, sir, thank you!" I rushed back across the lawn and climbed the stairs to the children's ward.

"You'll have to wait until the pediatrician gives permission to take her off the drip," the nurse greeted me. "He'll be here shortly."

"I'd advise you not to take this baby home," the pediatrician said later. "If we take her off the intravenous fluid, she will die tonight."

"And what happens if I leave her here?" I asked. "Will she live?"

The doctor looked down at the polished red cement floor. "No. She will die. We cannot save her."

"Then I will take my chances," I said. "Please give her to me."

The doctor nodded to the nurse, who went to the crib and began to detach the needle. "Promise me one thing," he said as he turned to go. "Promise that when she dies tonight, you will call the hospital and inform me."

"I promise," I said.

The nurse lifted the baby and placed her into my arms. On top she put the bundle of rags that had come with her.

"You will not die," I said to the little girl as I held her close. "You are going to live. I have a mommy for you, someone who loves you."

At the entrance to the hospital compound, I signaled a black-and-yellow taxi. "Coles Road," I said, and he took off through the narrow, crowded streets.

"Oh, God, please help her to live!" I prayed, "and help her not to have diarrhea until I can get her home!"

"I have a name for you," I whispered. "You are Jayarani. Jaya means victory, and rani is queen. You are my little victory queen. You are a beautiful baby, and I love you." There was no visible response, but Jayarani did not have diarrhea in the taxi!

When we got home, I called Philomena, an Indian lady who worked for us. "Go to the store quickly and get some diapers, baby formula, and bottles," I said.

Soon she was back. She mixed up some milk powder and brought the bottle to me in the bedroom, where I sat singing to Jayarani. The baby opened her mouth as if to cry, but not a sound came out. I stuck the nipple in her open mouth, but she did not suck.

So I shook a drop of milk onto her tongue and watched it roll back toward her throat. As it reached her throat, she swallowed. "Thank You, Jesus!" I cried. "Thank You! I know Jayarani is going to live."

It took two hours to feed Jayarani two ounces of milk, drop by drop. For forty-eight hours, either Philomena or I held her, talked to her, loved her, and fed her two ounces every two hours. And she never had diarrhea even once!

About sundown of the second day, Jayarani opened her mouth, and a little squeak came out.

"Thank You, Lord! Thank You." The tears ran down my cheeks as I held her close. "And thank you, too, Jayarani, for trying so hard. You are doing just great!"

Jayarani turned into a curly-headed, adorable little girl and today is a member of a loving, caring family in the United States.

Jayarani was the first baby admitted into Sunshine Children's Home, a home for abandoned children in Bangalore, India. Today, they have their own property, buildings, school, and farm. At the time of this writing, sixty-five children are being cared for under the direction of Rosette and Peter Davamony.

Sunshine Children's Home was begun in July 1979 in my spare bedroom. By Christmas of that year, we had twelve children and four cradles lined up in the center of our living room. It was begun with the sponsorship of Reach International in Berrien Springs, Michigan. Today, it is run under the auspices of the South India Union of Seventh-day Adventists and is supported by Asian Aid and other donors in Australia and North America.

Sunshine Children's Home is the culmination of an Eggs Expedition I took to Prayer Country in 1966. That was the year I wrote out my "Eggs" prayer and tucked it away in the back of a file-cabinet drawer. It went like this:

"Dear God, I feel so bad about all the abandoned babies I read about in the papers. I wish I could do something to save these babies, but I don't know how to get started. If You will send the babies to my doorstep, then I will find a way to take care of them."

The next morning I got up early and opened the front door, fully expecting a baby to be lying there on my steps, but there was none. I soon forgot about my prayer in the busyness of mission life and the excitement of becoming an adoptive mother of three Indian children. But all the time, my prayer lay there in the back of my filing cabinet, like a spiritual egg, just waiting to be hatched in God's own time.

In a recent move, I decided to clean out my files for the first time in twenty-six years! There on yellowing paper, I found my prayer for an orphanage. It wasn't my only request tucked away in that file. I was amazed as I read down the list and saw that every one of those prayers had "hatched" out. God had answered every one of my requests even though I had forgotten I had even written them!

Catherine Marshall talks about the "Eggs" prayer in her book *Adventures in Prayer*. She suggests that we turn our hopes and dreams into prayers and write them onto slips of paper cut into the shape of eggs to symbolize our willingness to let God "hatch them out" in His own time.

She further suggests that we hide those prayers in a safe place, perhaps between the pages of a favorite Bible, where they can be found at a later date.

Catherine Marshall had written out "Egg" prayers about her children. She tucked them away and forgot about them, until one day she came across the slips of paper in an old Bible. She, too, was amazed that a loving Father had fulfilled every single request.

If you have ever tried hatching eggs, you know that it takes just so long for the process to take place. There is really not much you can do but wait until the time comes for them to hatch.

David seemed to know about the principle of Eggs prayers when he wrote, "Wait on the Lord: be of good courage, and he shall strengthen thine heart: wait, I say, on the Lord."

"God's purposes know no haste and no delay," says Ellen White (*The Desire of Ages*, p. 32). We can bring our requests to Him, trusting Him to work things out in His own time.

Experience the tour

1. Spend several days thinking about your hopes and dreams for yourself, your family, and your church.

2. List them on a piece of paper and ask the Holy Spirit to guide you to eliminate any selfish requests that are not according to God's will.

3. Now write each prayer on a piece of paper and cut into the shape of an egg to symbolize your willingness to let God "hatch" it out in His own time.

4. Hide the prayers away in a safe place, showing your trust in God to do whatever He thinks is best with those prayers when the time is right.

5. Take them out after several months or years. You will be amazed at how God has been working for you!

6. Consider those prayers that have not yet been "hatched." Are they still a deep desire of your heart? Then put them back and wait. Evidently God's timing has not yet come.

7. Make a nest of eggs, one for each member of your family. Write the name of a loved one on each egg. Under the name, write one desire you have for that person. Turn over the egg and write a promise that you are claiming for that person. Put your Eggs prayers away and let them hatch.

8. Make a nest of goals for yourself. What kind of person would you like to be? What would you like to accomplish for God? Write one goal or dream on each egg. On the back of the egg, write a promise that you are claiming for yourself. Put your eggs goals away and let God hatch them in His own time.

9. Do a Bible word study on the word *wait*. Using a concordance, make a list of Bible verses in which *wait* or *waiting* is used. Read one each day. Read it in several versions. What does that verse have to say to you about your Eggs prayers? Write down the thoughts that come to you.

10. Divide a sheet of paper into three columns. In the first column, write the name of a Bible character who had to wait for an answer to his or her prayer. In the second column, list the request that was made. In the third column, put the length of time between the asking and the receiving.

TOUR THREE

The Promises Package

"W ould you like to adopt twin boys?" Ron asked.

I gripped the telephone receiver a little tighter, pulled out a chair, and sat down at the kitchen table. This was the moment I'd been waiting for all summer. We had come to the United States on furlough from India with a goal of finding a baby to adopt, and now we were offered two!

"They are newborns," he continued. "They are ours if we want them. Would you like twin boys?"

"Yes! Yes! Of course!" I pounded the table, frustrated that I was sitting in my mother's kitchen in Jackson, Ohio, while Ron was 2,500 miles away in Loma Linda, California. He'd gone there for speaking appointments while I had stayed home to do purchasing and packing for our scheduled return to India the first week of September. It was now mid-August.

My mind raced as I thought of all that must be done during the next three weeks to get twin boys ready for the trip to India. I felt like jumping on the next plane to California to get started!

"We don't have much time," I said. "How soon can we get them?"

"There's just one hitch." Ron's voice sounded so far away. In the living room, the TV was blaring out a commercial. A truck rumbled by in the alley next to the house. Someone was running a power mower. I strained to catch his next words. "We won't be able to go back to India now if we decide to adopt these boys. California law says that we must live here with them for one year before taking them out of the country.

"I'm willing to do that," Ron was saying, "but we need to make very sure that this is the right thing for us to do. I'd like for us to pray about it overnight. I'll call you tomorrow evening to see how we feel the Lord is leading. Don't you think we ought to do that?"

"I suppose," I agreed, but felt let down, disappointed. I didn't want any more delays. I'd already waited eleven years for this moment, and one more day seemed unnecessary. After we hung up, I went into our bedroom and knelt to pray. My prayer went something like this: "Lord, I want those boys so badly. You know how long I have waited. Surely You won't say No to me again."

My mind wandered back six years to our decision to adopt. We attended the required classes and had our interviews. Finally we were promised a baby. And then we got the call to India. First we were told there would be no problem, we could take the baby with us. Then, at the last minute, after the baby things were packed in our shipment, we were told that we'd have to stay in the United States for at least one year until the adoption proceedings were finalized.

We had accepted God's call to work in India. We felt strongly we should not back out, so we went without the baby. I thought surely the Lord would reward our sacrifice with the healing of my womb and the birth of a child, but He did not. During the next five years, I gave away all the baby things I had packed so hopefully.

Now, here was another opportunity, and I wanted those babies desperately.

"Please, God, show us Your will." I prayed because I had promised Ron, but my heart was not in it. Tears rolled down my cheeks as I looked up to the ceiling and begged, "Please let it be Your will for us to have those babies."

I listened, but God didn't answer. All I knew was that I wanted the babies. How was I supposed to figure out what God's will was in this situation? I lay awake most of the night thinking about it, but by morning I still had not heard God's voice or discerned His will.

About 9:00 a.m., the letter carrier came by to deliver a packet of books I'd ordered six weeks before. They were books on prayer written by Glenn Coon. Flopping down on the porch swing, I opened one of the books and began my first trip into Prayer Country using the Promises Package.

I read with excitement how I could know for sure that my prayers would be answered. "It's as easy as ABC," stated Coon.

A-ASK

A is for ask. "Ask, and it shall be given you; seek, and ye shall find; knock, and it shall be opened unto you" (Matthew 7:7).

Ask for something God has already promised to give you. Find one of the 3,573 promises in the Bible, one that names something you need.

B-BELIEVE

B is for believe. "What things soever ye desire when ye pray, believe that ye receive them, and ye shall have them" (Mark 11:24).

Believe that God keeps His word. Believe that He will not lie. Believe that with Him, all things are possible and He will surely do as He has promised.

C-CLAIM

C is for claim. Claim the promise as your very own. Kneel with the Bible open to the promise. Put your finger on the promise, and read it back to God. Say, "God, You said it, and I believe it. I now claim that promise and ask You to do what You have promised to do. And I thank You for doing it. Amen."

Returning thanks that I had already received the promised blessing, even though I couldn't see it, was the key. In doing this, I would be following the example of Jesus at the grave of Lazarus (see John 11:4) and the advice of Ellen White:

For any gift He has promised, we may ask; then we are to believe that we receive, and return thanks to God that we have received.

We need look for no outward evidence of the blessing.

The gift is in the promise, and we may go about our work assured that what God has promised He is able to perform, and that the gift, which we already possess, will be realized when we need it most (*Education*, p. 258).

It sounded so easy. I had to give it a try!

All I needed to do was to find one of those 3,573 promises that said, "Ron and Dorothy shall adopt twin boys from California." It wasn't there!

However, I did find one in James 1:5 that stated, "If any of you lack wisdom, let him ask of God, that giveth to all men liberally, and upbraideth not; and it shall be given him."

I knelt down and placed my finger on the promise and prayed, "Dear God, You have promised to give me wisdom if I will only ask. I'm asking. Please give me wisdom about Your will concerning the adoption of these twin boys. Should we adopt them and stay for a year or not adopt them and return to India immediately?

"I believe You will do what You say. I believe You will give me wisdom. In fact, I thank You for the wisdom that You are already giving to me, right now!"

And at that moment the word *car* popped into my mind, and I saw a picture of the car we'd been using for three months. If we were going back to India, we needed to sell it quickly. If we were staying to adopt the babies, we needed to keep the car.

We had tried selling it before Ron left for California, but no one responded to our ad in the newspaper. We took the ad out of the paper for the time Ron would be gone.

Maybe that is why it didn't sell! I thought. Of course! God knew about those twin boys and how we would need the car for the next year. I began to get excited! This was the answer I wanted! How "neat" that God would work it all out ahead of time! The Promises Package was really working!

"Lord, is this it?" I prayed. "Is this what You want us to do? Are we to keep the car and adopt the babies? Could the sale of the car be Your way of revealing Your wisdom?"

The phone rang. I got up from my knees to answer it.

"Do you have a car for sale?" a woman asked.

Now this was incredible. It wasn't even in the newspaper. How did she know?

"Yes, but it's not in very good condition," I hedged. "You might not want it. I think there is something wrong with the clutch and the carburetor, and maybe the starter and the brakes."

"My dad's a mechanic," she said. "Can we come over and look at it now?"

Within fifteen minutes, they arrived. They drove the car around the block. The man looked under the hood and checked this and that. "Nothing wrong I can't fix," he said. "How much do you want for it?"

We had bought the car for $850. Ron said we'd be lucky to get $600 for it. I don't know what possessed me, except that I did not want that car to sell! I said, "$925."

"We'll take it," he replied. "Will you accept a check?"

I nodded. I knew that God had showed me what He wanted us to do. Instead of feeling sad about losing the twin boys, I was excited to see how miraculously God had revealed His will when I used the Promises Package.

When Ron called that night, he shared how the Lord had also impressed him that we should turn down the adoption offer and return to India immediately.

As we look back, we can see that this was definitely God's leading. The next ten years were ones of exciting evangelistic growth in south India. And as a bonus, the Lord gave us three children, two boys and a girl, all beautiful Indian children, who are now grown and living in North America.

After that experience, the Promises Package became a regular map I used in my journeys into Prayer Country. For the first time, I wrote out a prayer list, which I kept in my Bible. Beside each need I wrote a promise that met that need. Each day I began reading those promises back to God, claiming the promise as my own, and thanking God for doing what He had promised.

There were thirty-three requests on that original prayer list. Within six months, I had visible answers to every one of those requests. I was amazed. In that six-month journey through Prayer Country, I had more answers to prayer than in the thirty years before I began using the Promises Package.

Experience the tour

1. Read the following texts to strengthen your faith that God will keep any promise He has made: Numbers 23:19; Joshua 23:14; Psalm 89:34; Isaiah 46:11; Jeremiah 33:3; Matthew 24:35; Hebrews 6:18; 10:23; 2 Peter 3:9.

2. Choose one of the nine verses in step 1. Copy it onto a 3 x 5–inch card. Place it where you can see it several times during the day. Let it remind you that God can be trusted to keep His promises.

3. Make a list of your needs. Include your spiritual, social, mental, and emotional needs as well as your physical needs.

4. Choose one of the needs. Try to think of a promise that meets that need. Use a concordance to help you. Will one of the following promises help? Proverbs 3:6; Isaiah 41:10; 49:25; Malachi 3:10, 11; Luke 11:13; Philippians 4:13, 19; James 1:5; 1 John 1:9.

5. Ask. Ask God to give you the thing that He has promised. Be specific in your request.

6. Believe. Put your finger on the promise. Read the promise back to God and tell Him that you believe He will do as He has said He will do, since He is a God who does not lie.

7. Claim. Thank God that you already have the thing that He has promised. Rejoice in His goodness in giving you that gift.

8. Repeat steps 4 through 7 for each need on your prayer list.

9. Check off each item as you see the visible evidence of God's answer to that prayer. You may want to write a date or other brief notes as each answer is received. Try doing this with a different-colored pen.

10. Go on a promises hunt. Get a red pencil (or any other color you choose) and read through the Bible, looking for promises that are meaningful to you. Underline the promise in the color of your choice. In the margin, write one or two words that identify what the text promises.

11. Make a notebook collection of promises. At the top of the page write such words as: *forgiveness, joy, protection, financial needs, wisdom, patience*, etc. As you locate new promises, copy

them into your notebook under the correct heading. Alphabetize the headings for easy reference.

12. Make a card-file collection of promises. Copy special promises onto 3 x 5–inch index cards. Put one word at the top right-hand corner that tells you the topic of that promise. Alphabetize the promises by topics. This will help you find a promise instantly to fit your needs.

TOUR FOUR

The ACTS Map

A fire crackled in our wood stove. Matt, our golden retriever, sprawled across my feet. I nestled against the velvet of my favorite chair and looked out at a winter wonderland.

Yesterday it had snowed all day, a soft, fine, gentle snow. The bareness of birch and aspen had turned into a featherlike loveliness. Fir branches bowed low. Everything was white. Even the sky was a luminous silver, the low morning sun hidden behind the majestic peaks of the Chugach Mountains that surrounded our home in Anchorage, Alaska.

That morning I had shoveled a foot of snow from the decks and railings, but already another inch had piled up. Stellar jays, magpies, chickadees, and nuthatches busied themselves at the feeders, making little tracks in the fallen snow.

It's as though the whole busy world has come to a stop, and no one knows when it will start again, I mused.

The house had also come to a halt. The furnace was out, the phone was dead, the yard light wouldn't turn on, and the garbage disposal was on the blink. The furnace needed a new valve, the repairman had informed us, and it would be another three days before one would arrive from Seattle. Meanwhile, we could keep warm with an electric heater and the wood stove.

The phone had been out for four days, and I'd been told that maybe someone would come tomorrow to fix it. With no communication from the outside world, two writing projects were on hold for lack of information.

"What perverseness has caused everything to stop working

at once?" I asked Matt. "All this makes me want to stop working too!"

He opened one eye to look up at me and wagged his tail as if to say, "So, why don't you stop, then? Follow my example."

I sat there for a long while watching the birds on the deck, enjoying the stillness and beauty of the morning. What lesson is there in this for me? I wondered.

"Be still, and know that I am God." The words of Psalm 46:10 came to mind. And in the quietness I could almost hear God say, "Dorothy, you need to spend more time with Me. You need to slow down to enjoy our friendship."

I glanced at the book on the end table that I'd been reading—*Too Busy Not to Pray*, by Bill Hybels. Now would be a good time for a journey into Prayer Country following the ACTS Map recommended by Hybels.

ACTS is an acrostic. The letters stand for Adoration, Confession, Thanksgiving, and Supplication. Using the ACTS Map as a guide, I took out my journal and wrote the following prayer.

A-Adoration. Lord, I adore You for Your loving care for all creatures in this white wilderness. You see each little chickadee nestled under the snow-laden spruce boughs. What a marvelous God You are! I'm amazed that You not only have time for the smallest of Your creatures, but that You also want to spend time with me.

C-Confession. Lord, forgive my impatience, my fretting about my circumstances, my lack of trust in You. I confess, Lord, that I've been too busy. Forgive my hustle and bustle that has left You out.

T-Thanksgiving. Thank You, Lord, for the snow and for my warm, cozy home. Thank You for the companionship of Matt. Thank You for work to do and time to do it.

S-Supplication. Please help me to finish all that needs doing today. Give me a creative mind and a cheerful heart. Please help me to be patient. Help me to slow down.

Snow continued to fall. Power lines broke under the accumulation of snow and ice. A power outage left our home in early-morning blackness. Now *nothing* in the house worked! We lighted emergency candles and kerosene lamps. We cooked porridge on the wood stove and had a romantic breakfast by candlelight.

After Ron had gone to the office, I sat in my chair by the fire to meditate and pray. The verse in Scripture that came to me was Psalm 27:1, "The Lord is my light." I meditated on the verse, then wrote in my journal another ACTS prayer.

> **A-Adoration.** Lord, I come to You as a moth comes to the flame, as a man lost heads toward the light. Life would be so dark, so hopeless, so confusing, so cold, without You! I love You, Lord, for You are my Light, my Joy, and my Warmth.
>
> **C-Confession.** I confess my own darkness without You, my willingness at times to sit in darkness, when I could have the Light. Lord, I have experienced the truth of Ellen White's words, "The darkness of the evil one encloses those who neglect to pray."
>
> **T-Thanksgiving.** Thank You, Lord, for the direction Your Word gives to my life. I'm grateful that my writing project is nearly finished. The light of inspiration came from You. Thank You for the warmth of Your love, the glow of Your presence.
>
> **S-Supplication.** Lord, I long for my children to walk in Your light today. Draw them close to You with the warmth of Your presence.

My journals are peppered with ACTS prayers. It's encouraging now to go back and read them. It's a map I turn to often because it is so rewarding.

Benefits

I see three major benefits that come from using the ACTS Map:

1. It slows you down. In a chapter called "Slowing Down to Pray," Hybels likens our minds to car motors, revved up to ten thousand revolutions per minute by the duties and demands of daily life. The adrenalin flows and we are caught up in the intense pace of modern life, with little time left for quiet moments with God. Writing out an ACTS prayer reduces your RPMs from ten thousand to five thousand.

2. It helps you to focus on your relationship with God. No relationship can flourish if all you do is say Hi! as you run from one task to another. To get to know someone, you must spend time with them, sharing your activities and dreams and listening to them share theirs. Love takes time to grow.

The ACTS Map slows you down long enough to enjoy a meaningful exchange of ideas with God in meditation and prayer.

3. It puts balance into your prayer life. For too many years my prayers were pretty heavy on the "Give me" side. What relationship would grow if there were only requests for help, with no words of admiration and appreciation and no expressions of honest self-disclosure?

An ACTS prayer makes sure that we balance our prayer requests with words of adoration, gratitude, and self-disclosure. The ACTS prayer makes sure that we treat God as the person that He is and not a machine that spins out Prayer Country souvenirs.

How to compose an ACTS prayer

Adoration. Adoration centers on the character of God. We express our love and admiration for Him because of who and what He is. One way is to zero in on one word that describes God's character. We might write our paragraph of adoration centered around His majesty, wisdom, or creative power. Perhaps we are most impressed that day by His compassion or never-failing love.

Confession. Open your heart to God and admit the sins you have committed. Be honest and specific. It's only as we focus on individual sins that we can come to grips with our sinfulness and our need of a Saviour.

Instead of simply naming the sin, such as selfishness, give an example of that sin. "Lord, today I pouted because Ron was asked to sit on the platform for church, when I wanted him to sit with me. Lord, forgive me for my selfishness."

Thanksgiving. Pause a moment to say Thank You for specific blessings the Lord has given you. The very act of gratitude will make you feel good. On my fifty-fourth birthday I made a list of fifty-four things for which I was thankful. I started out wondering if I could find that many blessings but discovered it would have been easy to list fifty-four more!

"Our devotional exercises should not consist wholly in asking and receiving. Let us not be always thinking of our wants and never of the benefits we receive. We do not pray any too much, but we are too sparing of giving thanks. We are the constant recipients of God's mercies, and yet how little gratitude we express, how little we praise Him for what He has done for us" (*Steps to Christ*, pp. 102, 103).

Supplication. I pray about my needs in different categories: physical, emotional, social, mental, financial, professional, and spiritual. Then come the needs of people in my personal network: my husband, children, grandchildren, relatives, friends, the pastors' wives in our conference, and others who have asked to be on my prayer list.

Sometimes I've come to God feeling like a beggar because my list was so long. With the ACTS prayer, I feel more like a beloved friend. Having prayed a balanced prayer of adoration, confession, and thanksgiving, it feels natural to share my needs with my Friend as well.

Through the ACTS Map I have experienced that prayer is indeed "the opening of the heart to God as to a friend" (*Steps to Christ*, p. 93).

Experience the tour

1. Draw three horizontal lines across a sheet of 8 ½ by 11–inch paper to divide it into four sections. At the top of each section, write one letter of *ACTS*.

2. In section A, write a paragraph of adoration to God. Admire Him for who and what He is. Tell Him why you love Him. Tell Him what you appreciate about Him.

3. In section C, write a paragraph of confession. Be specific rather than general. Tell exactly what acts you did that were

wrong. What thoughts did you think that were sinful? Ask God's forgiveness for what you have confessed.

4. In section T, write a paragraph of thanksgiving. Express your gratitude for specific things the Lord has done for you—prayers answered and blessings bestowed.

5. In section S, write a paragraph about your needs. What is it you want Him to do for you, your family, and your friends today? Be as concrete and specific as possible.

6. Now go back and read your prayer to God. Then sit quietly for a few moments to listen for what He wants to say to you.

7. On a sheet of 8 ½ x 11–inch paper, write the alphabet vertically down the left side. Use the back if you run out of room. Set a stop watch or timer for five minutes. See how many words you can list that describe God. Try to get at least one for each letter of the alphabet. Use this list to guide you in the adoration part of your prayer for one month. Use words that start with a different letter each day.

8. Get a wicker basket. Place in it objects that will remind you of something for which you are thankful. For instance: house keys—my comfortable house; leash—my dog Matt; marriage license—thirty-three years of marriage; binoculars—the ten new birds I've added to my life list; an airplane ticket—a recent vacation; passport—freedoms I enjoy; etc. Keep going until your basket is full. Then take out one item each day and use that as the basis of your paragraph of thankfulness.

9. On a sheet of 8 ½ by 11–inch paper, write the letters of your name in a vertical position. Beside each letter think of things or people who begin with that letter for which you feel genuine gratitude. Use that for your thanksgiving paragraph on one day.

10. Find a psalm that expresses your feeling of adoration, confession, or thanksgiving. Copy portions that appeal to you as part of your ACTS prayer.

TOUR FIVE

The Text Tour

L et's take a break," I called ahead to Ron. "I need to catch my breath."

"OK!" he answered. Followed by our dog Matt, Ron left the trail, heading for a large rock in the midst of a field of pink heather.

"Just look at that view!" Ron exclaimed as I plopped down beside him.

My eyes followed his hand as it swept across the expanse of a long, narrow valley flanked by rugged mountains that still held snowy remnants of an Alaskan winter. Clumps of lupine and forget-me-nots reflected blue from the sky. White and yellow anemones lined the alpine path and filled in open spaces between mounds of heather. Here and there chocolate lilies and red columbines added their touch of color.

Dozens of Wilson's warblers with their jaunty black caps and bright yellow coats flitted among willow thickets. Here and there, golden-crowned sparrows sat on the tips of dwarf trees repeating their three-note song that sounds for all the world like "Three Blind Mice."

A shrill whistle startled us. Looking around, we saw no one. Then it came again, from somewhere to our right. We searched the rocks and found him at last, a marmot sunning himself on a ledge.

"Look!" Ron said, nodding toward our left. "Look at that!"

At first, I saw only the long, rocky trail over which we had come. Raising my sights, I saw what he meant. An eagle seemed to be floating his way up the valley. In a matter of seconds, he covered the distance it had taken us three hours to achieve.

Oh, to be an eagle! I thought. His feet don't hurt and he'll have no aching muscles tomorrow.

To mind came the words of Isaiah 40:31: "They that wait upon the Lord shall renew their strength; they shall mount up with wings as eagles; they shall run, and not be weary; and they shall walk, and not faint."

Later I wrote in my journal: "I'm thinking Isaiah 40:31 should be my text for the year. It fits this stage of my life perfectly! I will repeat the text every day and claim its promises of new strength and energy."

For the next several months, that verse became my special text, the statement of my innermost spiritual desires. I purchased stickers of the text and stuck them inside cupboards, on closet doors, the bathroom mirror, the refrigerator, and the bulletin board above my desk.

I bought pictures of eagles to frame, an eagle bookmark for my Bible, and eagle stationery. I even bought a book about eagle habits. I learned everything I could about these majestic birds and tried transferring the principles I learned into my daily life.

For almost a year, that one text was the focus of my quiet time with God. Taking the text apart, I studied one word at a time, beginning with the word *wait*. I got out my concordance and made a list of all the texts that speak about waiting on the Lord. I took them, one at a time, and made that one text the center of my meditation for the day. I read it in several versions, trying to understand what it meant, and then endeavored to translate that into my personal experience.

A listening God

One day, as I meditated on Psalm 40:1, "I waited patiently for the Lord; and he inclined unto me, and heard my cry," I wrote in my journal:

This describes a *listening God*. Like a puppy dog I'm waiting at God's door. Patiently I wait there until the time is right. He comes, leans down to me, and listens to

my cry, the cry of my need, the cry of my soul. He under-
stands it all. He opens the door and lets me into His presence. What a warm, beautiful thought to begin my day!

Give God a chance

A few days later the verse was Proverbs 20:22: "Say not thou,
I will recompense evil; but wait on the Lord, and he shall save
thee." I wrote that morning:

> Lord, today You are telling me, "Don't *fight* with evil
> in your life. Instead, *focus* on Me. Wait on Me. Give Me
> a chance. I will right all wrongs. I will deal with evil-
> doers. I'll save you, justify you, and lift you up. Leave the
> battle to Me, OK?"
>
> I responded, "OK, Lord. You know all about a situa-
> tion in my life right now in which I have been unjustly
> accused. I want to defend myself and get even, but I
> won't. Today I choose to leave the battle with You."

Expect God to work

Psalm 37:7 and 9 really struck home during another morning's devotions. "Rest in the Lord, and wait patiently for him:
fret not. . . . Evildoers shall be cut off: but those that wait upon
the Lord, they shall inherit the earth." I wrote:

> Dorothy, you want to get in there and do something:
> organize, control, make things happen. But I am saying
> to you, "Expect Me to care for your problems, and I will.
> Wait on Me. Don't try to do it alone. The reason you don't
> wait is that you don't really expect Me to do, so you do it
> yourself. I'll care for you, Dorothy; just wait patiently."

On eagle's wings

Exodus 19:4 promises, "I bare you on eagles' wings." In
response I wrote:

> This gives a picture of helplessness, inability, weak-
> ness on my part. Strength, ease, soaring, height, and

adventure all come when I'm "on eagle's wings."

I love the independence, strength, and remoteness of the eagle. It excites me. But I am not the eagle, You are! What I need is simply to let You "bear me up on eagle's wings." All I do is rest and cling. You do the soaring and flying and getting me where I need to be. I see that as a true picture of my need right now. Lord, bear me today, for I have no strength or desire to fly on my own. Thank You! Today I will soar "on eagle's wings"!

Renewing your mind

For several days, I focused on the word *renew*. "They that wait upon the Lord shall renew their strength."

At the same time, I was reading through the book by Florence Littauer, *Freeing the Mind From Memories That Bind*. About my thoughts at this time I wrote:

> For several weeks I've been bothered with memories of my past. Lord, I know You have forgiven me, for I have asked. But the memories keep coming back to haunt me. I wish, Lord, You could burn away those memories from my mind as the sun burns away the cold morning mist from the land.

The Lord gave me His answer in Romans 12:2: "Be ye transformed by the renewing of your mind," and Colossians 3:10: "Put on the new man, which is renewed in knowledge after the image of him that created him." I wrote:

> The more time I spend beholding Christ, the more of His characteristics I will possess. The knowledge I need is a knowledge of God. As I think on Him, my mind will be renewed, cleansed, changed.
>
> Lord, come into my mind, every cell, every memory recorded there. Wash my mind clean! Renew each nerve ending and brain cell. Purify and take control and make my thoughts Your thoughts. As I spend time with You, renew my mind.

How renewing takes place

I discovered more about how God's renewing takes place as I meditated on Psalm 103:5. Here God promises that "thy youth is renewed like the eagle's." In the preceding verses, He lists six things we can do to hasten this renewal: remember His blessings, accept His forgiveness, experience His healing power, accept His redeeming grace, recognize His kindness and mercy, and live by His health principles.

I wrote: "That is wonderful! It gives me much to think about. Lord, where am I lacking?"

The source of strength

While studying the word *strength* I got a new thought from The Living Bible translation of Philippians 4:13: "I can do everything God asks me to with the help of Christ who gives me the strength and power." My prayer of response was:

Lord, I hear You saying to me, "Everything you attempt to do, Dorothy, I haven't asked you to do. Instead of trying to be a marvel and a wonder and do all things, why not be content to do all things that I ask you to do. When I ask, then I will give the strength you need."

But, Lord, that's hard to know sometimes. Give me wisdom to know when You are speaking and when it is just my own ambition or someone else's expectation.

The Text Tour

For a year's journey through Prayer Country via the Text Tour, I am indebted to my friend, Ruthie Jacobsen, who shared the idea with me one day on the phone. She, in turn, got it from Fred and Florence Littauer.

Ruthie explained how she was using it with a small women's prayer group. She exchanged texts with each member of her group. Each day the women prayed for each other through their chosen Bible text, asking the Lord to do for that person just as He had promised to do. She told of the wonderful things that were happening through this method of prayer.

I decided to follow that plan with the pastors' wives in Alaska.

Beside each name, I wrote out the text that each had chosen as her text, the one that best expressed her needs at that stage of life. As I prayed for each of my friends, I read the text back to God and asked Him to do what He had promised in that woman's life. It was a beautiful experience that drew me not only closer to God, but to each of my friends.

To this day, I can't hear certain texts read without remembering those Alaskan friends with whom I walked the Text Tour through Prayer Country.

Experience the tour

1. Choose one text that summarizes your current needs and desires. More than anything else at this stage of your life, what is it that you need from the Lord?

2. Write your chosen text on a 3 x 5–inch card. Put it in a place where you will be able to see it often.

3. Memorize the text.

4. You may want to visit Christian bookstores to find plaques, bookmarks, wallet cards, and other items on which the text is printed.

5. If you are into crafts or needlework, you may want to design a wall hanging centered around the words of your chosen text.

6. On a piece of paper write down the main words of your text. For Isaiah 40:31, I wrote the words: *wait, Lord, renew, strength, eagle, wings, run, weary, walk, faint.*

7. Using a concordance, write down those texts that seem appropriate under each word.

8. Each day choose one text for your meditation. Read it from several different versions. Which one best speaks to you? Copy it.

9. If you have a commentary available, read what it says about your text. What new insights do you gain?

10. Does Ellen White use that text as the basis of a message? You will find a Scripture Index to her writings in the *Comprehensive Index to the Writings of Ellen G. White,* volume 1. Read something she has written based on that text.

11. Write out what you feel God is trying to tell you through

that particular text; then write out a prayer of response.

12. You may want to exchange texts with family members or close friends, using your chosen texts to pray for each other for a period of time.

TOUR SIX

The List Cruise

Y**ou've done a super job organizing the weekend," a guest speaker told me. "I've been to several women's retreats, but I've never seen a retreat leader so relaxed. How do you do it?"

"I've had a great team to work with!" I answered. That was true. We did have an excellent group of women who helped make the retreat happen.

But the real secret behind the organization was the lists. Each participant had a list of her specific duties to perform. I had spent hours on lists: shopping lists, seminar lists, menu lists, decoration lists, supplies lists, topics lists, speaker lists, mailing lists, name lists, thank-you lists, and prayer lists. Then I had lists of lists.

I have a choleric-melancholy temperament, which means that I am highly work oriented. It's important that I see everything that's going to happen down in black and white on a list. I can check off the items on the lists and feel in control.

I suppose that's why I enjoy a List Cruise through Prayer Country. The List Cruise puts everything on paper, where you can see it. As God answers your prayers, you can check off each item with the date and manner in which He worked. The List Cruise gives you proof of answered prayers.

Another beauty of the List Cruise is that it gives you a sense of control over the circumstances of your life. Your list represents a decision you have made. You may not be able to control the items on the list, but you can control your reaction to them. You have chosen to react with faith in God's power.

If you, too, enjoy making lists, you will find the following variations of the List Cruise a pleasurable experience.

The Omnibus Cruise

I first learned of the Omnibus Cruise from Morris Venden, although he doesn't call it that. In his book *The Answer Is Prayer*, Venden suggests that we make up five lists to present to God: our wants, our joys, our sorrows, our cares, and our fears. He bases this idea on a paragraph in *Steps to Christ*, page 100:

> Keep your wants, your joys, your sorrows, your cares, and your fears before God. You cannot burden Him; you cannot weary Him. . . . Take to Him everything that perplexes the mind. Nothing is too great for Him to bear, for He holds up worlds, He rules over all the affairs of the universe. Nothing that in any way concerns our peace is too small for Him to notice.

The idea captivated me. I laid aside the book and got out my journal. I made a list of everything I wanted—an IBM-compatible computer and WordPerfect's word-processing program, among other things. Next, I listed my joys—items such as my dog Matt and birds at my feeder.

I continued by making a list of the sorrows of my life, those things that make me cry. I put down the loved ones I had lost as well as current disappointments.

Next, I listed all my cares, those things that cause me to lie awake at night. These were the burdens I carried, the tasks that needed doing, the bills that needed to be paid. Here were listed my responsibilities in church, home, and community. Finally, I listed my fears, such things as a doctor's appointment and failure in a project.

My lists filled two pages of my blank book. Then I wrote a paraphrase of Ellen White's words in *Steps to Christ*:

> It was good to share those lists with You, Lord! Just to know that Your heart is touched by my sorrows and even by my utterance of them. That I can bring You everything that perplexes the mind. That nothing is too

great for You to bear. That nothing that in any way concerns my peace is too small for You to notice. There is no chapter of my life too dark for You to read, and no perplexity too difficult for You to unravel. No calamity can befall me, no anxiety harass me, no joy cheer me, no severe prayer escape my lips, but that You take an immediate interest! Wow! What a friend You are!

The Traditional Cruise

The traditional prayer list consists of a list of names. The special need of that person is usually listed as well: healing, a house, money for bills, courage to face life, comfort in mourning, wisdom, or protection. Some include a promise to claim for each person's need.

As each prayer is answered, a check is made beside the name or the need. Some people write in the date, time, and method God used to answer that request.

The Blessings Cruise

The first time I went on the Blessings Cruise was during a stressful move. It seemed that nothing was going right, and I was exhausted from trying to deal with my problems. I decided to give God a list of my trials.

I started in. Trial number one. Trial number two. About this time I could almost hear God say, "Come now, Dorothy! Do you only have trials? Haven't I sent any blessings your way?"

"Well, yes, I guess so," I admitted. "OK. For every trial I'll try to think of a blessing."

Blessing one. Blessing two. Trial three. Blessing three. Trial four. Blessing four. Blessing five. Blessing six . . . When my list was finished, I was amazed to see that I had only four trials and eleven blessings!

The Decision Cruise

I used this cruise when faced with the choice of two interesting jobs. I used a page of my journal to list the positive aspects of the first job: shorter drive, more prestige, better office, more money. Then I listed the negative aspects: less interesting, no experience in that field, tight control of management.

On the next page I listed the pros of the second job: interesting work, freedom for creativity, more responsibility, my background fits in, feel needed. The cons I listed included: traffic hassles, travel expense, small office, long hours.

For several days I prayed over those two pages of lists, asking God for wisdom. Finally, I wrote: "Dear Lord, thank You for making it clear which job I should take. I feel certain that I am exactly where You would have me to be!"

The Goals Cruise

This is a cruise I charter at least once a year. I set aside a morning for quiet meditation and prayer about the coming year. I put my year's goals into my journal under the following categories: physical, mental, social, family, spiritual, and professional.

I try to be very specific so that I can later measure those goals to see if I have reached them. It is also useful to write down what I will need to do to make those goals happen. Then I offer up the list to God and ask Him to give me the strength to reach the goals He has impressed me to write. Several times during the year I flip back to those goals to see how we are doing.

The To-Do-List Cruise

I often use a page of my journal to list projects I want to accomplish before a certain date. I offer this list to God for His scrutiny as part of a written prayer that goes something like this:

God, I have lots to do during the next two weeks. Here is what I am planning to do. Please help me to set my priorities. Which are the most important items to get done? Are there some projects I should not attempt now? Please show me what You would have me do. I'll be listening daily to Your voice nudging me about projects to drop and projects to add to my list.

The List Cruise is a practical application of Ellen White's suggestion:

Lay all your plans before God, to be carried out or given up, as His providence shall indicate. Accept His plans instead of your own, even though their acceptance requires the abandonment of cherished projects. Thus the life will be molded more and more after the divine example; and "the peace of God, which passeth all understanding, shall keep your hearts and minds through Christ Jesus." Philippians 4:7 (*Testimonies*, vol. 7, p. 44).

A List Cruise is not quick and easy. It takes time to write down lists and pray about each item on the list. It takes time to look up promises that apply to your needs. It takes time to listen for God's voice to guide you as you set goals and enumerate blessings. It takes time to search your heart and list all your wants, joys, sorrows, cares, and fears. Yes, it does take time, but isn't that what a journey into Prayer Country is all about—spending time with your Friend, the King of Prayer Country?

Experience the tour

1. Make five columns on a sheet of paper. Write one of the following words at the top of each column: *wants*, *joys*, *sorrows*, *cares*, and *fears*. Then write as many things as you can think of under each category. Each item must apply to you personally. Read the list to God as part of your prayer.

2. Get a blank book or notebook that will serve as your prayer journal. Make a list of those people for whom you want to pray. Beside each name write your prayer desire for them. Read over the names and your requests each day during prayer time. Carry the list with you and flip to it while you are waiting at a stop light, at an office, or in a queue. Take advantage of spare moments to pray for those on your list.

3. Make a list of your blessings. Write a short paragraph about each one. Present this to God in a prayer of praise and thanksgiving. Include trials if you wish.

4. Do you have a decision to make in the near future? Divide a sheet of paper into two columns: pros and cons. Write a list of the advantages and the disadvantages of the proposal. Commit the lists to God and ask Him to show you what you should do.

5. Set aside at least two hours for quiet meditation. Ask God to help you make a list of goals for the next twelve months. Consider physical, mental, social, spiritual, family, financial, and professional goals.

6. Make a to-do list for a day or a week. Write out a prayer that includes the list. Ask God to help you set priorities. Ask Him to show you what doesn't need doing. Are there other things He wants you to do instead?

7. Make a list of all the qualities of character you would like to have. Or do it this way: draw a tree; then draw circles inside the tree. On each circle write one of the fruits of a righteous life that you need to see growing in your experience. Ask God to send His Holy Spirit to produce those fruits in your daily experience.

8. Make a list of answers to prayers you have received. Go back in your life as far as you wish. Then read the list to God and thank Him for each one.

9. For one week keep a running list of little things that happen or that you see in nature which give you pleasure (examples: a child's smile, a warbler's song, a rainbow in a mud puddle, a call from a friend). Then offer that list to God in a prayer of praise and thanksgiving.

10. Make a book of lists. Divide a notebook into several sections. Keep a separate running list in each section. Some lists you may want to include: prayer list, praise list, thanksgiving list, goals list, wish list, quotation gems, best-thing-that-happened-today list, nature-joy list, and any other list you may want to keep. In my own book of lists, I include a list of books I've read; stories I've told, along with the date and place; writing ideas; and manuscripts I've sent to a publisher. Each of these lists at some time or other becomes a part of my prayer experience.

TOUR SEVEN

The Sanctuary Safari

I began my first Sanctuary Safari in a Ford Taurus on Highway 27 between Lansing and St. Johns, Michigan. In the winter of 1987, I used my half-hour commute to listen to tapes about Sanctuary Prayer.

The tapes were a gift from Carol Zarska, a classmate from my Mount Vernon Academy days. We had corresponded for more than twenty years, and I was aware that Carol's spiritual journey had led her back to school to study religion. I knew that she had experienced a revival in her life and was now sharing that experience with audiences around the country. I was pleased when she sent me a set of her tapes about Sanctuary Prayer, a route through Prayer Country that she and Michael Curzon had pioneered.

Step by step, Carol led me on a Sanctuary Safari. In my imagination, she took me to the sanctuary in the wilderness and walked with me through the rituals followed long ago by white-robed priests. I began to see that ancient service as more than symbols of a Saviour to come, as more than an outline of Christ's work in the heavenly sanctuary. I began to see in it a pattern to follow in personal worship.

The gate

Our first acts of worship as we enter the gate of the temple courtyard are praise and thanksgiving. "Enter his gates with thanksgiving and his courts with praise; give thanks to him and praise his name" (Psalm 100:4, NIV).

One morning this is what I wrote: "Lord, I praise You for Your faithfulness. You are someone I can count on!

"Thank You for the opportunity to visit my children. Thank You for the beautiful fall colors, that Ron is happy, that I have a golden retriever, for our cozy home in the woods."

My personalized expressions of thanksgiving may seem rather simple beside the great classics of praise, but I am encouraged to continue them by these words of Ellen White: "Every individual has a life distinct from all others, and an experience differing essentially from theirs. God desires that our praise shall ascend to Him, *marked by our own individuality*" (*The Desire of Ages*, p. 347, emphasis supplied).

The altar of sacrifice

Directly in front of us as we enter the courtyard is a large brass altar. It is here, morning and evening, that the priests offered a lamb, symbolizing Jesus, the Lamb of God. In my imagination I can see Jesus, my Substitute, dying on Calvary's cross for my sins.

Just as those wilderness worshipers long ago confessed their sins over the head of their sacrificial lambs, so I come to Christ in my sanctuary of prayer and confess my sins. I try to be honest with myself before God as I acknowledge specific sins and shortcomings, stripping away my pride and laying my soul bare before Him.

One morning, I wrote this prayer of confession:

> I told a lie to the inspector at the Canadian border. I said I was living in Jackson, Ohio, so my residence would match the U.S. license plate. I lied to save all the hassle of having to park and explain everything to a customs official, since Canadian residents aren't supposed to be driving U.S. rental cars into Canada.
>
> Lord, I know that You hate lying lips. This week the Sabbath School lesson just happens to be on honesty and integrity. I'm wishing now I had told the truth and suffered the consequences. Please forgive me. Make me a woman of integrity!

The laver

Between the altar of sacrifice and the door of the tabernacle we come to a brass washing bowl, where the priests cleansed themselves from the blood of the sacrifices.

It is here that I accept Christ's cleansing work on my behalf. By faith I can know for sure that the sins I have confessed have now been washed away.

At the laver I pause a moment and hear Jesus say to me, "Dorothy, you have confessed your sin, and I am faithful and just to forgive your sin of lying and to cleanse you from all unrighteousness" (see 1 John 1:9).

"Thank You, Lord, for Your cleansing power, Your forgiveness!" I respond. "How good it feels to be clean!"

The candlestick

Next we enter the first room of the tabernacle, the Holy Place. To our left, we see a seven-branched candlestick. The oil in the seven lamps represents the Holy Spirit.

Here we pause a moment and ask for the gift of the Holy Spirit to illumine our minds, to guide us in our prayer experience. We don't know how to pray as we should, but the Holy Spirit will come in response to our invitation. As we train our minds to listen to His voice, He will lead us to promises we need to claim, sins that we ought to confess, and people for whom we should pray.

The table of shewbread

On the north side of the Holy Place, directly across from the candlesticks, is the table of shewbread. Here the priests placed two piles of flat bread each Sabbath day. The bread represents Christ, the Bread of Life, and His Word, which feeds us spiritually.

It is here that I pause and ask the Holy Spirit to guide me to a personal message. I pick up reading in the Bible wherever I left off the day before, continuing through one or two chapters until I come to a verse that stands out as God's message to me. Sometimes I underline the verse. Often I copy it into my journal.

Sometimes my message is a promise. At other times it is a message of reproof, and I may need to pause a moment for another prayer of confession. At still other times, I sense there is something God wants me to do. I make notes of people I need to call, letters I need to send, articles I should write, or changes in my to-do list.

The altar of incense

On the western side of the Holy Place is the golden altar of incense. Here the priest offered prayers of intercession for the people, and it is at this point in my Sanctuary Safari that I bring my petitions to God. This is where I present my prayer list.

It was at the altar of incense that the priest came closest to the mercy seat, to the very presence of God, which dwelt between the cherubim of the golden ark. Ellen White describes it this way:

> As the inner veil of the sanctuary did not extend to the top of the building, the glory of God, which was manifested above the mercy seat, was partially visible from the first apartment. When the priest offered incense before the Lord, he looked toward the ark; and as the cloud of incense arose, the divine glory descended upon the mercy seat and filled the most holy place, and often so filled both apartments that the priest was obliged to retire to the door of the tabernacle (*Patriarchs and Prophets,* p. 353).

In Sanctuary Prayer, I try to picture myself before the very throne of God. I try to imagine His brightness and glory, His love and compassion. I come boldly before His throne because of the incense that represents Christ's merits accompanying my requests. Because of His righteousness, I know that my worship is acceptable and that my prayers have been heard.

A typical experience

One morning while praying in the Holy Place of my personal sanctuary, the Holy Spirit led me to pray for a dear friend who was going through a difficult experience. As I thought about her specific wilderness journey, I thought of the promise of Isaiah 43:19: "I will even make a way in the wilderness."

Although my bookmark was at Matthew 20, the place I had planned to start reading, I felt nudged by the Holy Spirit to read the whole of Isaiah 43 instead. I found it full of promises that fit my needs as well as those of my friend. Here was food from the table of shewbread. In my journal, I copied those promises and claimed each one for my friend in my prayer of intercession at the altar of incense.

Then I felt impressed that I should write her a letter and send a check to help with her needs. I copied out the promises, personalizing each one with my friend's name, and enclosed them in my letter.

A few weeks later, I got a note from her that said, in part, "Thank you for the money and that very special letter. I've read it over several times. It has helped me so much! I thank God for you."

The Most Holy Place

Once each year, on the Day of Atonement, the high priest entered the Most Holy Place. There in the direct presence of God, everything was made right.

As I spend time with Jesus, my High Priest, who is interceding now for me in the Most Holy Place, He will make everything right in my life, past as well as present. He wants to search my mind and motives to reveal hidden sins. He wants to teach me more about Himself, flooding every corner of my heart with His joy, peace, and victory.

Experience the tour

1. **The gate:** Offer praise and thanksgiving as you start your prayer journey. Compose your own prayer or read a psalm or praise poem from the hymnal.

2. **The altar of sacrifice:** Imagine Christ, the Lamb of God, hanging on the cross of Calvary, paying the price of your sins. Make specific confession of sin.

3. **The laver:** Here you pause to accept the forgiveness and cleansing that Christ has provided. Thank God for keeping His promises in 1 John 1:9; Isaiah 1:16-18; and Psalm 103:10-12.

4. **The candlestick:** Ask for the Holy Spirit as you pause

beside the golden lampstand. Ask Him to guide you into truth as you study God's Word and present your requests.

5. **The table of shewbread:** Spend time meditating on a portion of Scripture. Ask the Holy Spirit to impress you with the messages that are ones you need. Underline those messages or copy them into a notebook.

6. **The altar of incense:** Picture yourself standing before the throne of God, bringing your requests before His mercy seat. Present your petitions boldly, for your prayers are mingled with the merits of Christ, making them acceptable. Spend some time listening for directions that the Holy Spirit may give.

7. **The Most Holy Place:** While you wait in God's presence, ask Him to search your heart and motives and to reveal to you what He wants to teach you.

8. Study "The Tabernacle and Its Services" in *Patriarchs and Prophets*, pages 343-358, along with Exodus 25-40 and Leviticus 4 and 16. Try to imagine what the sanctuary in the wilderness was like. Picture yourself in prayer, walking through that tabernacle with Jesus, your High Priest.

9. Color code Psalm 27. You will need the following colored pencils: blue, green, red, purple. Let the colors stand for the following:

blue – what God is like, His character;

red – a promise;

green – a command, something God wants you to do;

purple – a reference to the sanctuary.

You may want to try this with other portions of Scripture as you spend time in the Holy Place at the table of shewbread.

10. Read through the books of Psalms and Revelation, underlining in purple each reference to the sanctuary or any of its services. Your Sanctuary Safari will begin to take on new meaning as you notice the many references that speak of its importance.

TOUR EIGHT

The Bouquets Vacation

The bouquet of wine red roses and delicate white baby's breath made a striking picture reflected in the dresser mirror. Its subtle fragrance filled our bedroom, making me feel cherished by my husband. He had given the flowers to me for our anniversary.

During the next few days, the unfolding petals spoke to me a thousand times the words Ron had said when he presented the bouquet, "I love you, sweetheart! You are precious to me."

That feeling of love and belonging is also mine whenever I receive a "bouquet" from Jesus in Prayer Country. I feel wonderfully cherished each time I discover one of His "bouquets."

A geese bouquet

I had just written five pages of frustration accumulated during our move from Anchorage, Alaska, to Abbotsford, British Columbia. For the sixteenth time, I was having to put a new house in order, find my way around a new neighborhood, get acquainted with a whole new set of people, and find my niche in the scheme of things. I felt like everything that could go wrong had gone wrong on that particular day, so I wrote it all out and handed it to God—a list of my frustrations.

"Lord, where are You leading me in all of this?" I cried. "It's so hard, and no one seems to understand!"

"Honk! Honk! Honk!" came the answer from somewhere nearby. I looked out the window to see a flock of Canada geese gliding low over the vacant lot next door for a landing on Mill

Lake. What a picture they made with mountains, trees, and clouds perfectly reflected in the still waters of the lake.

I could almost hear God saying to me, in a paraphrase of Matthew 6:26: "Behold, Dorothy, the geese; for they sow not, neither do they reap, nor gather into barns; yet your heavenly Father feedeth them. Are you not much better than they?"

"Yes, Lord, oh, yes!" I whispered.

In my mind the dialogue continued with a paraphrase of Matthew 6:33: "Dorothy, Dorothy, put the building up of My work in British Columbia first in your life, along with your daily time with Me in devotions, receiving My righteousness, and all of these things [clothing, food, shelter, friends, all of your needs] will be supplied."

"Thank You! Thank You!" I wrote in my journal. "What an understanding, caring God You are!"

Whenever I hear geese honking or see them flying overhead, I feel cherished, reminded again of that message of love from Jesus, one day's "bouquet" from God.

A bouquet in a storm

On another day I looked out my upstairs study window on a stormy scene.

Fall leaves raced along the wet street toward the yellow curb at the dead end, jumped over the curb, and came to a sudden halt at the fence between us and the vacant lot next door.

Dark clouds billowed over the mountains and flew across the sky as though late for an important appointment farther east.

Gale-force winds made trees bend and sway gracefully, sometimes fast, sometimes slow, doing an aerobic dance standing in place. Trunks bent but did not snap; branches shook but did not fall. How patiently they danced with their roots holding them firmly in place. In sunny weather, they would stand tall again.

I thought of the dance of the wind, a stormy ballet performance of the trees, grass, and flowers. What a beautiful sight when you are safe behind a thermopane of glass, surrounded by protecting walls. It might not seem so beautiful if I were a tree participating in the dance of the cold, biting west wind, I thought.

"God, is that what Your people look like to You and the rest of the universe?" I wrote in my journal. "You see us, Your people, bending, swaying, but not breaking before the bitter winds of temptation and trouble. As we stand firm, dancing in place as the winds whip us back and forth, do we appear beautiful in Your sight? I rather imagine we do."

As though going along with my metaphor, understanding my thoughts, God seemed to whisper James 1:2, 3 to me: "Count it all joy when ye fall into divers temptations; knowing this, that the trying of your faith worketh patience."

I paraphrased it to read, "Count it all joy when you dance the dance of the winds. Your performance is a beautiful sight to those who watch from afar."

In the midst of a very real time of trial in my life, God had once again sent me a "bouquet" to make me feel understood, loved, cherished.

An evening bouquet

One Friday morning, I bounced out of bed the minute the alarm went off. It was winter in Anchorage, and the sun would set by 3:30. I'll have to skip morning devotions, I thought. There will be plenty of time for meditation tonight around the fire after sunset. Now I've got to get going. I'll have to go double-time as it is to get everything done by sunset.

I started a load of wash while the water heated for porridge. The rest of the morning, I raced around the house trying to accomplish two days' work in half a day. By noon I was ready to run errands.

I got to the conference office just in time to stuff letters in the mailbag that was already sitting by the door awaiting the letter carrier. From there I headed down the mountain to the supermarket.

On the way, it suddenly dawned on me that I'd put an unaddressed envelope meant for Kathy Dufer, the conference accountant, in the mail pouch. It contained a check that would not be delivered without stamp or address. By now, the pouch had gone!

I rushed home with the groceries to finish my Sabbath-meal preparations. As I pulled into the driveway, I saw a letter lying on the seat that I had promised to take to the post office. It was our mortgage payment and must not be delayed! I turned around and headed back to town.

At the post office, I forgot to put the car in park. It rolled backward, hitting a truck. That took time exchanging names, phone numbers, and license numbers. By now, the sun had set.

I gave up on any preparations for Sabbath dinner and decided to add a log to the fire and collect my thoughts. I turned the draft dial at the back of the wood stove to the highest position and opened the door. With a flash, flames shot out, singeing off my eyebrows and eyelashes and scorching my face. I slammed the door shut and ran to splash cold water on my burning face.

At last, I settled down in my rocker by the fire to write in my journal: "Lord, what a mess! I've done at least four stupid things today. Would things have been different had I taken the time this morning to talk with You? Probably so. I'm sorry. Please forgive me.

"No, I don't think You punished me. You just let life take its course. I made all of those stupid mistakes because I was under stress, trying to be a superwoman in my own strength.

"If I had only taken time to spend with You this morning, I would have found the calmness I needed to set priorities and live my life a little more sanely today.

"Things could have been so much worse. Thank You for sparing me, for being with me even when I didn't ask, for suffering with me in all of my stupidity."

And then, in that moment, when I felt so disgusted with myself, I received a "bouquet" from Jesus. I seemed to hear His whisper above the crackle of the fire, a paraphrase of Hebrews 13:5: "I will never leave you, Dorothy, nor forsake you, even on days like today when you rush headlong into trouble without Me."

That "bouquet" of words made me feel loved in spite of my stupidity and neglect.

What a friend God is! I thought. Imagine sending a message of love at a time like this!

The bouquet idea

My friend, Ione Richardson, gave me the idea of calling personalized messages from God, paraphrased to fit my situation, "bouquets." She is the author of a devotional diary of inspiration and personal praise called *Bouquets, With Love, Jesus*.

The book contains one hundred texts selected by Ione with a paraphrase she has made during her own quiet time with God. There is then a space to put down my own paraphrase, how it relates to my experience, and my own prayer of praise or commitment in response to the bouquet.

The three bouquets I have listed above fit into this pattern: The Word, my paraphrase, my experience, and my prayer. I'll share another "bouquet," including the headings, to show you how easy it is to take a Bouquets Vacation in Prayer Country.

A bouquet of fruit

The Word. "The fruit of the Spirit is love, joy, peace, long-suffering, gentleness, goodness, faith, meekness, temperance" (Galatians 5:22, 23).

My paraphrase. "The fruit of the Spirit doesn't ripen overnight. Just as there are seasons for fruit growing, there are seasons of the soul. Dorothy, if you will wait through this winter, accepting the pruning knife and the biting elements, then spring and new life will come. If you are patient, the fruits of joy and peace will once more appear in your life."

My experience. Someone had criticized me severely. I wrote in my journal: "Right now I feel like a barren fruit tree. All the sap has gone. I'm brittle, cold, whipped about by winter winds of censure and criticism. I feel suddenly that I am a liability to Ron and the work, worthless, good for nothing but kindling to be thrown into the fire. I feel hurt, teary, exhausted. But in this verse I see a little hope. If winter comes, can spring be far behind?"

My prayer. "Lord, thank You for hope and the promise of spring. Just help me to survive the winter winds and the hurt of the knife. Give me love for the person who has criticized me. Help us to become friends."

From the day I received this "bouquet" from Jesus, I felt once again worthwhile, someone who was deeply loved and cherished in spite of mistakes I had made.

Experience the tour

1. Divide a sheet of paper into four horizontal sections. At the top of each section, write one of the following phrases: *the Word*, *my paraphrase*, *my experience* or *my plan*, *my prayer*.

2. Choose a Bible verse that seems to have a special message for you at this moment in your life. If you can't think of one, open to Psalms and read until you find something.

3. Read the verse in several different versions. Choose the one you like best.

4. Copy the verse into "the Word" section.

5. Write your own paraphrase of the text. Just put down what you feel the verse is saying to you about your current life situation. Put your name into the paraphrase if it will help it seem more personal. Imagine that this is what Jesus is saying to you.

6. Next write down something of your experience to which this verse speaks, or write how you want to act now as a result of what the verse is telling you.

7. Follow this with a prayer of praise, thanksgiving, or supplication. This is your response to Jesus for the bouquet of love He has just given you.

8. Read the following quotation from *My Life Today,* substituting the word *bouquets* for "glad springs" and "precious truths."

> Make the promises of God your own. Then when test and trial come, these promises will be to you glad springs of heavenly comfort. . . . The heart that is stored with the precious truths of God's Word is fortified against the temptations of Satan, against unholy thoughts and unholy actions (p. 28).

9. Underline each day's bouquet in red in your Bible. Beside it write the date. Sometime when you feel discouraged, leaf through your Bible and enjoy your bouquets.

TOUR NINE

The Journaling Trip

L ife was too busy for prayer. I was commuting forty miles a
day, teaching, writing, presenting seminars, and traveling
around the conference with my husband.

My prayers were on the run. I listened to tapes in the car and
fell asleep on my knees at night. I knew I was neglecting my
inner life, but I didn't know what to do about it.

Then Ron left for a week of speaking appointments. For the
first weekend in many months, I had time on my hands. I
scanned our bookshelves for something to read and pulled out
Gordon MacDonald's *Ordering Your Private World.* Fascinated
that his experience paralleled my own, I stayed up most of the
night to finish the book.

My first journaling experience

MacDonald recommended keeping a journal. I began that
very day. My first entry says:

> Wonderful Sabbath! Time to get away from people
> and think. I need very much silence in which to order
> my world, my thoughts. I need time to think through
> my motives and get in touch with myself and with God.
> I'm excited about journaling.

The next day I started a Bible-study program, researching
Bible women. I began with Mary and Martha, reading everything I could find in Scripture, the *SDA Bible Commentary,* and

The Desire of Ages. About Martha I wrote:

> Very anxious, troubled, workaholic, Type A personality, driven, left-brained, practical, not perceptive. I see much of myself in Martha. It's OK to be a Martha, but I need to get my priorities right (Matthew 6:33).

A day later I commented: "Martha thought Jesus needed her, when in reality she needed Jesus."

The following day I noted:

> I need less anxiety for things that pass away and more for those that are eternal. All of my Martha qualities (dependability, energy, hard work, organization, concentration, and responsibility), if sanctified by Christ, can make my life a power for good.

Then came my first journal prayer: "Lord, please do it. Sanctify my abilities. Help me find time to sit so that You can work!"

God answered that prayer. Journaling has brought a revival to me spiritually, has helped me understand myself, and has showed me how to organize my life. Before I started journaling, one minute was the average length of my prayers. Now I seldom spend less than half an hour. Often an hour or more passes, and it seems but a moment.

What is a spiritual journal?

A spiritual journal is more than a diary of happenings. It is a record of my reactions to those happenings. It is a record of my spiritual progress, my thoughts, ideas, insights, and prayers. In it, I dialogue with my innermost self and with God.

What do you put in a journal?

It is entirely up to you. Anything. Everything. Here are some things that go in my journals.

Daily activities. I jot down where I was, who I was with, and what I did. I might include the interesting comments of a grandchild, a good joke, or new birds I found for my life list.

Reaction to something that happened. Following is my reaction to our visit to the Haystack Monument in Williamstown, Massachusetts. It was built on the spot where Samuel Mills and his four friends had a prayer meeting under a haystack when caught in a rainstorm. Here the American missionary movement was born. I wrote:

> I felt choked up, a sense of wonder and gratitude for what those youth did. Sensing the sacredness of that moment, the seriousness of their commitment, and a wonder at what God can do with so little, Ron and I knelt facing the monument.
>
> Ron prayed, rededicating our lives to God's worldwide cause of taking the three angels' messages to every nation, kindred, tongue, and people. We asked God to use us to carry on the spirit of those five young men, to allow us a part in inspiring the church for missions. It was a beautiful moment, a stirring experience I will never forget!

Messages from God. Some years, I read the Bible through. One year, I read the five-volume Conflict of the Ages series by Ellen White. I read until God speaks to me, underlining the verse or paragraph and copying it into my journal. Often I paraphrase the verse and personalize it with my name as though God is speaking directly to me.

One day I felt overwhelmed by the many tasks I had to accomplish. Deadlines were approaching and new obligations kept intruding. I began to panic. I drew a sketch of a stick man drowning in the ocean. Across the sketch I wrote my prayer, "Help! Lord! I'm drowning, and I've no strength to swim!"

I then opened my Bible and began reading Acts 27 where I had left off. Of all things, it was about Paul's shipwreck. My message came in verse 44: "They escaped all safe to land."

I wrote: "Lord, it seems You are saying to me, 'Just as I was able to see Paul safely to land, so I can see you, Dorothy, safely to land too. You will not drown!' "

My prayers. I write out my prayers. Sometimes it is an

ACTS prayer or perhaps a list of my wants, joys, sorrows, fears, and concerns. It might be a prayer of thanksgiving or praise. It could be a Palms Up, Palms Down prayer or a prayer to claim a promise. All of the prayer patterns covered in this book have found their way at some time into my journal.

Answers to prayer. The beautiful thing about recording prayers is that you can so readily see when each prayer is answered. I often go back and write in the answer and date in a different color of ink along the margin.

For instance, on August 28, 1989, I wrote: "Lord, I'm feeling a bit discouraged about my writing. Please, I need a little encouragement from someone soon."

That evening I drew a star beside the prayer and wrote: "Got it. From five different sources. Amazing! Thank You, Lord."

Beauty spots. I look back over the day and try to remember something in nature that gave me real joy, a snapshot of beauty that I don't want to forget.

On June 17, 1989, beside a page of pressed wildflowers, I wrote:

> Red and yellow columbines growing with purple lupines in a splash of sunlight. Sitting on a wooden bridge over a gurgling mountain stream. Cool breeze, tiger swallowtails, abundance of bright green fiddleneck ferns. I felt like my cup was filled to overflowing with Your presence, Lord, with Your beauty! Thank You!

Quotes and notes. I often write a brief summary of a sermon I've heard or a chapter I've read. I often put in quotes or my reaction to something I've read.

An example is a statement by Catherine de Haeck quoted in *Celebration of Discipline*: "All in me is silent and . . . I am immersed in the silence of God." I wrote:

> Oh, how I long to be immersed in the silence of God for just a little while, to have all the voices within me silent. There are so many voices: voices of pain, desire, family, career, friends, expectations, demands, accusa-

tions, opportunities, work to be done. Lord, amidst all of this noise, grant me the experience now and then of being immersed in Your silence. Hush all other voices and give me moments of peace in Your presence.

Goals. At the beginning of each year I write out my goals, using the following categories: physical, mental, social, spiritual, financial, family, and career. Sometimes, I list goals for a week or a month in the form of a to-do list. From time to time, I refer back to these goals to see how I am doing.

Special treasures. These may be leaves gathered from a nature walk, a ticket stub to a concert, a note from a friend, or the corner of a paper napkin from a special celebration. Sometimes I paste in a poem or draw a sketch.

Three bright red leaves of a wild geranium picked on a hike are accompanied by the following notes: "Hiked Glen Alps in the rain. Leaves bright and beautiful in spite of gray skies. Thank You, Lord! I think there is a message in the leaves for me."

Nature meditations. After a woodland walk searching for birds, I wrote:

Oh, to be an eagle, majestic, soaring high above the mundane problems and perplexities of life. I'd like to be an eagle sitting on a wind-swept crag high above the pollution and smog of human pettiness, but I am not an eagle.

I'd settle for being a swallow, graceful, beautiful, quick. They seem so happy at their swallow parties on telephone wires. I might even be a swallow at San Juan Capistrano, famous, acclaimed for my beauty, travels, and dependability, but a swallow I am not!

It seems to me that I am a plain, simple chickadee whistling to myself in the branches of an alder tree, hanging clumsily upside down in my efforts to do what has to be done, repeating the song of my life over and over again. Like the chickadee, I find it hard to sit still, always busy, determined, driven to accomplish all I can in one day.

The chickadee is everywhere—in parks, yards, woods, and fields. While she's nothing for spring and summer bird-watchers to get ecstatic over, what a joy she brings when seen on a naked branch on a winter's day. She still sings the same little song, cheerful in spite of the circumstances. She is not jealous of her more famous summer neighbors who travel the world. She's content to put down roots, to take life as it comes, both good and bad, to weather the storms, to outlast the gale.

I'm glad I'm a chickadee. I think I'll collect pictures of the chickadee so that I can remind myself to be happy for what I am, to be content where God has placed me.

Memories. One Christmas, Ron and I tried to remember the highlights of each Christmas we had spent together. I recorded each one in my journal: where we were, who shared dinner with us, what was special about that Christmas.

One Christmas is special because Ron broke his arm. Another stands out because I saw forty-five new birds to add to my life list at San Blas, Mexico. One Christmas is memorable because of the blizzard we experienced in Portland that left thousands of people without power. We spent the day setting up an emergency shelter and making soup to feed the homeless. It's fun to look back and remember how God has led.

Experience the tour

1. Buy a blank book or a spiral notebook. Write a paragraph about why you want to journal. Write a prayer asking God to guide your journey. Below are some exercises to try.

2. **Suitcase exercise.** Imagine you are putting items into a suitcase. These items will help your children remember you when you are gone. What items would you choose? Write a paragraph about each item to explain what it would reveal about you.

3. **Awareness exercise.** Choose a spot to relax and observe. Describe everything you see, hear, smell, taste, feel. What emotions does the scene arouse? Does God have some lessons there for you?

4. **Daily events.** Write about a recent event in your life. How do you feel about it? Did you learn any lessons from it? What did it tell you about yourself? Did you see God at work in the incident? If you had it to do over again, what would you do differently?

5. **Scripture meditation.** Choose a Bible verse. Read it in several versions. Copy the version you like best into your journal. Paraphrase and personalize the passage. What is God saying to you in this verse? Write a prayer of response.

6. **Beauty spot.** Go for a nature walk. When you return, open your journal and paint a word picture of something beautiful you want to remember.

7. **Memories.** Where were you living when you were five years old? Describe your house and your favorite room. How was the house heated? Who was the center of emotional warmth? Recall something you did or something that happened to you at that age (if no memories come, choose a different age).

8. **Clock exercise.** Draw a clock. Put in the numbers, but no hands. Ask yourself the question, "What time is it in my life?" Draw the hands to show that time. Write a prayer about what you want to do with the time you have left.

9. **Omnibus list.** Make five lists to present to God: my wants, my joys, my sorrows, my cares, and my fears (see tour six).

10. **Palms Prayer.** Write a Palms Down, Palms Up prayer (see tour one).

11. **ACTS Prayer.** Write a prayer in four parts: adoration, confession, thanksgiving, and supplication (see tour four).

TOUR TEN

The PART PLAN

The PART PLAN, a variation of the Journaling Tour, is the ultimate prayer vacation for the highly organized person. Instead of the diary format, you use a notebook with dividers for each step of your prayer journey.

The two words *PART* and *PLAN* form acrostics for the eight division headings and represent the two-way communication of an ideal journey into Prayer Country.

PART describes communication going from you to God. The four letters of PART stand for the four aspects of a balanced prayer: **P**raise, **A**dmit, **R**equest, **T**hank.

PLAN outlines God's communication with you. The four letters of PLAN stand for four ways God can speak to you: **P**assages, **L**istening, **A**wareness, and **N**otes.

My PART

P - Praise. Copy a psalm or write a praise poem of your own on one page of the Praise section. Date your entry. The next day, skip a space and write a new love letter to God.

Praise expresses your feelings toward God because of who He is, not for what He does for you. Praise is an admiration of His character and an expression of your love to Him. In this part you say, "I love You, Lord, and here is why."

This is a favorite praise psalm:

> I will praise you, O Lord, with all my heart; I will tell of all your wonders. I will be glad and rejoice in you;

I will sing praise to your name, O Most High (Psalm 9:1,
2, NIV).

A - Admit. On a page of the Admit section, write out a
confession of your sins. Look back over the past twenty-four
hours and ask God to show you where you have failed Him. Be
specific in your confession. Then open your heart to receive His
cleansing and forgiveness. If your confession involves a sin you
have committed against someone that needs to be made right,
make note of it in the Listening section of the notebook.

We can be sure that God is willing to forgive:

He that covereth his sins shall not prosper: but
whoso confesseth and forsaketh them shall have mercy
(Proverbs 28:13).

If we confess our sins, he is faithful and just to forgive
us our sins, and to cleanse us from all unrighteousness
(1 John 1:9).

Search me, O God, and know my heart; test me and
know my anxious thoughts. See if there is any offensive
way in me, and lead me in the way everlasting (Psalm
139:23, 24, NIV).

R - Request. Draw a vertical line one inch from the left-hand
side of your page. This column will be used to date your requests.
Draw a vertical line one inch from the right-hand side of the
page. This column will be used to date the answer received. In
the middle column, list your requests. Don't hesitate to list your
wants as well as your needs. Also include your intercessory
prayer for others. God wants to hear our requests.

Delight yourself in the Lord and he will give you the
desires of your heart (Psalm 37:4, NIV).

My God shall supply all your need according to his
riches in glory by Christ Jesus (Philippians 4:19).

You do not have, because you do not ask God (James 4:2, NIV).

T - Thanks. Put in today's date and write a thank-you note to God. Express your sincere appreciation for blessings sent your way, gifts given, trials permitted, and prayers answered. This is the part of your devotions where you give an offering to God, the gift of a thankful heart.

Be joyful always; pray continually; give thanks in all circumstances, for this is God's will for you in Christ Jesus (1 Thessalonians 5:16-18, NIV).

Giving thanks always for all things (Ephesians 5:20).

Offer a sacrifice of thanksgiving (Amos 4:5).

God's PLAN

P - Passages. Here you record powerful passages of Scripture that speak to you. Jot down messages you get from God during Bible study. Read through the Bible, chapter by chapter and book by book, looking for promises or admonitions that God has placed there for you.

When you find a verse that touches your heart, stop to look it up in other versions and in the *SDA Bible Commentary*. What was the author's purpose in writing that verse? What does it mean to you, now? Write down your thoughts about this verse.

You may wish to paraphrase the passage, putting into your own words the meaning it holds for you. Include your name in the paraphrase.

If you limit yourself to one text per page, you can later file these according to the Bible book or topic. After several years, you will have your own commentary. Writers, speakers, and teachers find such a file invaluable in future creative work.

L - Listening. Take time to listen for God's voice. Sit quietly for a few minutes and wait for the Holy Spirit to speak. Ask Him to reveal His thoughts and plans for your life. Write down impressions that come to you. Maybe He will impress you with a verse of Scripture, someone you need to call, something you need to do, someone who needs your prayers, or a confession you need to make. Test your impressions against Scripture. God will never tell you to do something that disagrees with His written Word (see Isaiah 8:20).

> Thine ears shall hear a word behind thee, saying, This is the way, walk ye in it (Isaiah 30:21).

> The Lord confides in those who fear him; he makes his covenant known to them (Psalm 25:14, NIV).

A - Awareness. Become aware of lessons God wants to teach you in nature. Spend some time contemplating a part of God's creation. Let your heart thrill with the beauty of a rainbow or wonder at the flight of a swallow. Walk by the sea and sense its power or sit beside a mountain stream and let it calm your soul.

> Nature and revelation alike testify of God's love. . . . "God is love" is written upon every opening bud, upon every spire of springing grass. The lovely birds making the air vocal with their happy songs, the delicately tinted flowers in their perfection perfuming the air, the lofty trees of the forest with their rich foliage of living green—all testify to the tender, fatherly care of our God and to His desire to make His children happy (*Steps to Christ,* pp. 9, 10).

Everything in nature can be an object lesson in life. Take the time to look and enjoy. Write down the object lessons you see. With practice, you can learn to find a parable wherever you turn in garden, field, mountain, or stream. Oceans, insects, storms, and crustaceans all have a message to give. Try to find something beautiful or interesting in nature to record each day. If you sense a lesson for life, write it down; if not, just thank God for the beauty He made for you to enjoy.

N - Notes. Here you will include the notes you make of sermons or seminars. Take your notebook with you to church, retreats, and camp meetings. Date the page and make note of the speaker. Learn to listen for the outline of the main points. Jot down Scripture references. Reading over these messages at a later time will fix the truths in your mind. Taking notes will increase your ability to concentrate as well as clarify the message the Holy Spirit has for you in each presentation.

In this section, you may also want to make brief notes on books you read. Copy quotations or ideas that you want to remember. If you disagree with an author, use your notebook to list your arguments.

Notebook variations

Becky Tirabassi suggests the PART acrostic in her book *Releasing God's Power*. She has published *My Partner Prayer Notebook*, which uses the letters *L-M-N-O-P* for God's PART of her notebook prayer experience. The letters stand for: **L**istening, **M**essages, **N**ew Testament, **O**ld Testament, **P**roverbs. Under these headings she records blessings she receives from meditation, reading, study, or sermons. Her plan is to read one chapter from Proverbs, the New Testament, and the Old Testament each day.

Ann Ortland describes her notebook prayer journey in *Disciplines of the Beautiful Woman*. The sections she uses are: calendar, goals, Bible study, disciples, husband, neighbors, couples, sermons, and prayers. Included in these sections are all her prayer concerns as well as a record of her devotional life and witnessing activities.

Gordon MacDonald describes two sections to his notebook. The first section is his journal, the record of his spiritual progress, his prayers and interaction with God. The other section contains his prayer list. Interspersed among his prayer list are quotes he writes in from his current reading. He doesn't even use dividers. Instead he begins journaling from the front of a notebook and listing his intercessory prayer concerns from the back of the notebook. When the two sections meet, he begins another notebook.

Bill Hybels also has two sections to his notebook. In the first section, he journalizes about the previous day. He writes down what happened and his reflections on that twenty-four-hour period. In the second section, he writes out his prayers.

The PART PLAN is only one way to take a notebook journey through Prayer Country. You can have as many or as few sections as you choose. Experiment until you find what works best for you. The neat thing about a notebook is that you can add or delete sections to your heart's content.

It is not necessary to write in all eight sections each day. They are there to form a pattern in which you can fit your day's devotional experience.

Experience the tour

1. Get a looseleaf notebook, paper, and eight section dividers.

2. Write one of the following words on each divider tab: *praise, admit, requests, thanks, passages, listening, awareness, notes.* Turn back in this chapter for suggestions on what to write in each section. Remember, you don't have to write something in each section every day. Adjust the plan to your own devotional needs.

3. Other sections you may want to include are: to-do list, goals, calendar, books I have read, ideas for articles I want to write, stories I have told (sermons I have preached), and dates to remember (birthdays, anniversaries, etc.).

TOUR ELEVEN

The TRIALS Trail

Near Point is part of the majestic Chugach Mountains that encircle Anchorage, Alaska. Come with me now to the rocky trail that winds up its slope. It is June, and bright clumps of purple lupine, red columbine, and blue forget-me-nots give us an excuse to pause on our climb. Chocolate lilies, bluebells, and anemones blend into a patchwork design of springtime mountain beauty.

The climb is a hard one with many trials along the way—swampy areas, steep pathways, rushing streams, tired muscles, and weary, aching feet. But when we arrive, we know it was worth it.

Behind us, Anchorage glistens beside sparkling Cook Inlet. Snowcapped mountains edge the horizon. The day is clear, and the sight of Denali (Mt. McKinley), North America's tallest mountain, causes us to gasp. It's hard to believe that it is seventy miles away by plane, five hours by road.

Sometimes life is like the trail to Near Point. It is a painful uphill climb with muddy sections and problems as pressing as a mountain stream that must be crossed. The next time difficulty looms before you like a mountain, why not walk the TRIALS Trail through Prayer Country? Like the PART PLAN, TRIALS is an acrostic. Each letter represents part of a plan to overcome obstacles and problems that life serves you.

T - Thanks. Thank God for your problem. It is part of His plan to use your trial to His glory. He knows the glorious vistas that await you at the end of your uphill struggle.

He sees that some have powers which may be used in the advancement of His work, and He puts these persons upon trial; in His providence He brings them into positions that test their character and reveal defects and weaknesses that have been hidden from their own knowledge. He gives them opportunity to correct these defects and to fit themselves for His service (*Patriarchs and Prophets,* pp. 129, 130).

R - Request. Request God to show you the weaknesses and defects of character that He wants to remove from your life. Ask Him to show you the purpose of your trial, the lesson He wants you to learn.

He shows them their own weakness, and teaches them to lean upon Him; for He is their only help and safeguard. Thus His object is attained. They are educated, trained, and disciplined, prepared to fulfill the grand purpose for which their powers were given them. When God calls them to action, they are ready, and heavenly angels can unite with them in the work to be accomplished on the earth (*Patriarchs and Prophets*, p. 130).

I - Invite. Invite the Lord to walk with you through your trial. He will help you over the rough spots and guide you as you face forks in the trail. Alone, the climb seems impossible; with Him it is a joy.

He calls them away from human influences and aid, and leads them to feel the need of His help, and to depend upon Him alone, that He may reveal Himself to them. . . . He who will do this has the faith of Abraham, and will share with him that "far more exceeding and eternal weight of glory," with which "the sufferings of this present time are not worthy to be compared." 2 Corinthians 4:17; Romans 8:18 (*Patriarchs and Prophets*, p. 127).

A - Affirm. Affirm your faith. Declare your trust in God and His promises. Like Job, say, "Though he slay me, yet will I trust in him." Tell the Lord that You are determined to keep your faith during this trial, no matter how difficult your life may become.

Follow the example of Habakkuk, who wrote:

> Though the fig tree does not bud and there are no grapes on the vines, though the olive crop fails and the fields produce no food, though there are no sheep in the pen and no cattle in the stalls, yet I will rejoice in the Lord, I will be joyful in God my Savior (Habakkuk 3:17, NIV).

L - Lean. Lean on the "everlasting arms" of the King of Prayer Country, the one who walks the TRIALS Trail with you. He is a fellow hiker who will "never leave you, nor forsake you."

> God leads His children by a way that they know not, but He does not forget or cast off those who put their trust in Him. . . . He teaches them to lean upon Him (*Patriarchs and Prophets*, pp. 129, 130).

S - Surrender. Surrender yourself and your situation to the Lord. Stop trying to figure out what to do; rather, hand it all over to Him to work out as He sees best. He will show you what you should do.

> The very trials that task our faith most severely and make it seem that God has forsaken us, are to lead us closer to Christ, that we may lay all our burdens at His feet and experience the peace which He will give us in exchange (*Patriarchs and Prophets*, p. 129).

My experience

I first discovered the TRIALS Trail while reading chapter 11 in *Patriarchs and Prophets*, "The Call of Abraham." I found myself identifying with Abraham and Sarah in the uprooting God required. Moving is a trial I have experienced a good many times as the wife of a pastor and church administrator. More than once I have given up a job I enjoyed immensely to follow where God called. While these calls usually meant advancement for Ron, they meant a move backward in my career.

I read with interest, "Many are still tested as was Abraham. . . . They may be required to abandon a career that promises wealth and honor, to leave congenial and profitable associations, and separate from kindred, to enter upon what appears to be only a path of self-denial, hardship, and sacrifice" (*Patriarchs and Prophets*, pp. 126, 127).

Exactly! I thought. I know that feeling of rootlessness, of frustration at being a professional having to start from scratch wherever we move. It seems so unfair to be the one having to make those adjustments, and I've been tempted at times to complain about the trial I have to bear.

I also have felt the loneliness of leaving behind "congenial and profitable associations, and separat[ing] from kindred." It's hard to be far away from the support of family. It's difficult for a person of melancholy temperament such as I to reach out and make new friends.

I know what it feels like to enter upon "what appears to be only a path of self-denial, hardship, and sacrifice." Every move brings its own sacrifice and financial hardship as I go for months without work until something opens up. And why is it that when we move, our house doesn't sell within three days (with a tidy profit) as in the stories of others whom God has called?

Yes, I could identify with Abraham and Sarah's trials. Perhaps it was time that I walked the TRIALS Trail into Prayer Country instead of feeling so sorry for myself. It really has made a difference as I have embraced the trial, walking the trail in prayer. Let me illustrate with something from a recent journal:

T - Thanks. Lord, I thank You for our move. Looking back, I can see how You led all the way. This is where You want us to be. Thank You for making that clear. The happiest place on earth for me is right here in the middle of my confusion, because that is where You want me to be.

R - Request. Lord, we're feeling the pinch. Living costs are high, and I have no work yet after six months. I've done a lot of writing, but little has sold. What do You want me to learn from this experience? I hear You saying to me: "Dorothy, you have a very independent nature; you need to depend on Me alone. You rely too much on your own abilities and talents. You need to trust Me more."

I - Invite. Lord, You are so right! Forgive my self-sufficiency. Come walk through this trial with me. I cannot handle it alone. I need You to guide me, to help me find a job, to help me be outgoing enough to make new friends. I feel helpless to do these things on my own.

A - Affirm. Lord, I affirm my trust in You and my faith in Your promises. You are a God of integrity, One I can count on to keep Your promises. You have promised in Philippians 4:19 to supply all of my needs: friends, career, fulfillment, courage, and finances. You will provide food, clothing, and money for the mortgage. I believe that You will do what You have promised.

But even if things take a long time to work out, and though no one wants to buy the manuscripts I write, and though I get no job, nor any checks come in the mail, though I have to do without many things and people do not understand my difficulties, yet I will rejoice in You, Lord. I will be joyful, for You are my God and my Saviour!

L - Lean. Lord, I have nowhere to go but to You. Take my hand and help me over the hard places of this move. Give me patience for the long climb up the mountain. Don't let me fall.

And I hear You say to me, "Dorothy, fear not, for I am with you. Be not dismayed, for I am your God. I will strengthen you; yes, I will help you. I will lift you up with My right hand."

S - Surrender. Lord, just now I lay all of my concerns about this move at Your feet. Take away my worry about a job and where the money will come from to pay our bills this month. I lay all my talents at Your feet as well. I'm willing to use them or not as You see fit.

It's amazing the way God works when we walk through our trials in prayer with the King of Prayer Country! Below are only two answers to prayer that came during my numerous trials of transition.

Finding a friend

Soon after our move from Oregon to Michigan, I was alone for a weekend. On Friday evening, I sat at the piano playing old familiar hymns, inviting Jesus to walk the TRIALS Trail with me, finding in the music a practical way to lean on Him. When I came to "I Want My Friends to Pray for Me," tears filled my eyes, and I couldn't see to play through to the end of the piece.

"Oh, God!" I cried. "I don't have even one friend in this new place to pray for me. Please, Lord, I need a friend! I'm so lonely."

The next day, I opened the mailbox to find a card from Muriel, a woman at a nearby church where Ron had preached. We had shared lunch and the afternoon with her and her family. The card said, "I feel impressed to write you a note and let you know that I'm praying for you. I'd like to be your friend."

Getting Muriel's letter was like sudden sunshine on a patch of lupines along a mountain trail. How precious was God's gift of a friend!

Finding a house

We were moving from Michigan to Maryland and had three days to find a suitable house. At the end of the first day, I tossed and turned on the motel mattress, unable to sleep. At last I got up and wrote in my journal:

> I am tired, taut, and tense from the trials and tribu-
> lations of house hunting. We found three, but none is
> satisfactory. Lord, I am thankful that in the midst of
> my perplexities of finding a house and a new job I have
> Your promises. You will never leave me nor forsake me.

You are powerful enough to meet my need. I believe You care about every detail of my life and that You can do abundantly above all that I ask or think. I need more than a house and a job; I need patience and a calm spirit. I need Your peace. I need You! I cast all my care on You; I rest now in You. Thank You, Lord. I can sense Your presence with me. I feel Your power, comfort, and calmness. I have Your peace. I can sleep.

The next day we covered a radius of twenty-five miles in three states, looking through seven newspapers. There were only two possibilities. By the time we called, both had been rented. Tears. Hurt. Fear.

"God has something better for us," Ron tried to assure me. "So let's be thankful that those houses are gone."

I knew he was right, but it wasn't easy. That night I struggled to sense God's presence on the TRIALS Trail. It was difficult to be back to zero.

On the third day I wrote: "Found house! Praise the Lord! It is better than any house we've seen so far. Why was holding on to faith such a struggle?"

We signed the lease in time to catch our flight to Lansing. On the ride back, I praised the King of Prayer Country for His goodness in the midst of our trial. He had walked the trail with us. There was still the matter of a job, but I knew He'd take care of that as well.

That wasn't the end of our trial. It was eight months before I got a job, but when I did, it was one of the most exciting of my career. Meanwhile, I did a lot of writing. Three books prepared during this waiting period have now been published. Perhaps more important were the lessons of faith I learned, the character insights I received, and the spiritual growth I experienced.

The next time a trial comes your way, I challenge you to walk the TRIALS Trail. You may be surprised to discover what a pleasant journey it can be!

Experience the tour

1. What is your trial? On a sheet of paper finish this sen-

tence: "My trial is . . ."

2. Write the letters of the word *TRIALS* vertically, down the left-hand side of your paper. Write a one- or two-sentence prayer that fits into each section, such as:

T - Thanks. Thank God for your trial.

R - Request. Request Him to show you what He wants you to learn from this experience. If He brings a weakness to your mind, write it down.

I - Invite. Invite Jesus to walk through the trial with you.

A - Affirm. Affirm your faith in God and His promises.

L - Lean. Lean on Jesus as you go through the trial. Turn to Him often to discuss your problem and receive strength.

S - Surrender. Surrender your situation and yourself to God. Allow Him to deal with you however He sees fit.

3. Divide a sheet of paper into two columns. In the first column, list trials that you have experienced. In the second column, list how God helped you through each trial. When you are finished, praise God for the many times He has seen you through a wilderness experience.

4. Read "The Call of Abraham" in *Patriarchs and Prophets*. Look for the following:

a. Seven reasons why God permits trials.

b. Four responses we should make to our trials.

5. Make a list of trials you have experienced. Alongside each trial, write at least one lesson you learned from that time of trouble.

6. Joseph is one who walked the TRIALS Trail through Prayer Country. Instead of rebelling against his misfortunes, he turned his trials over to God and asked for His presence to sustain him in his troubles. As a result, what lessons did Joseph learn from his trials? Read chapter 20 of *Patriarchs and Prophets*. Make a list of the lessons Joseph learned on this route.

TRAVEL TIPS

Travel Tips:
A to Z

Here are some lessons about prayer that didn't fit into any of the Prayer Country tours but are still important to remember.

Angels

Angels are the communication link between heaven and earth. They are God's agents sent to answer our prayers.

> Heavenly beings are appointed to answer the prayers of those who are working unselfishly for the interests of the cause of God. The very highest angels in the heavenly courts are appointed to work out the prayers which ascend to God for the advancement of the cause of God (Ellen G. White Comments, *SDA Bible Commentary*, vol. 4, p. 1173).

> The angels of God are ever passing from earth to heaven, and from heaven to earth. The miracles of Christ for the afflicted and suffering were wrought by the power of God through the ministration of the angels. And it is through Christ, by the ministration of His heavenly messengers, that every blessing comes from God to us (*The Desire of Ages*, p. 143).

Answers

God always answers prayer. Sometimes He says Yes; sometimes He says No; and sometimes He says Wait.

> When we do not receive the very things we asked for, at the time we ask, we are still to believe that the Lord hears and that He will answer our prayers.... When our prayers seem not to be answered, we are to cling to the promise; for the time of answering will surely come, and we shall receive the blessing we need most. But to claim that prayer will always be answered in the very way and for the particular thing that we desire, is presumption. God is too wise to err, and too good to withhold any good thing from them that walk uprightly. Then do not fear to trust Him, even though you do not see the immediate answer to your prayers (*Steps to Christ*, p. 96).

Business

Prayer is a business. It is writing a check on the bank of heaven; it is balancing the ledgers of life with the riches of eternity. Too often we treat prayer as a pastime, a hobby, or an emergency exercise, when in reality, it is a business that demands our best energies and organization.

"All who have walked with God have viewed prayer as the main business of their lives," states Richard Foster in *Celebration of Discipline*, page 34.

> Prayer and effort, effort and prayer, will be the business of your life. You must pray as though the efficiency and praise were all due to God, and labor as though duty were all your own. If you want power you may have it; it is waiting your draft upon it. Only believe in God, take Him at His word, act by faith, and blessings will come (*Testimonies*, vol. 4, pp. 538, 539).

Not a bad business deal.

Conditions

"To every promise of God there are conditions." "The conditions met, the promise is unequivocal" (*Education,* pp. 253, 258).

In his book *Too Busy Not to Pray*, Bill Hybels lists the following conditions for answered prayer: regularity, earnestness, persistence, confession, reconciliation, selflessness, a caring attitude, and faith.

Morris Venden, in *The Answer Is Prayer*, suggests the following conditions: realize your need; ask for help; no cherished sin; faith in God; perseverance; a spirit of forgiveness; go where prayer is made; unceasing prayer; prayer and work; ask in the name of Jesus; and thanksgiving and praise (see pp. 61-75).

Doubt

Doubt is Satan's most useful tool, the first one used in the Garden of Eden. Doubt is so effective because it drives a wedge between us and God; it keeps us from prayer and Bible study.

Doubt and faith are not opposite ways of looking at prayer. Rather, they are opposite ways of relating to a Person. Doubt says, "God didn't give me what I asked for in prayer. He doesn't really love me. He is a liar." Faith says, "My purpose in prayer is to build a relationship with God. I don't understand why He answered the way He did, but I trust Him to know what is best. I want God more than I want answers."

Enemy

The good sometimes becomes the enemy of the best. Anything that keeps you from prayer is an enemy. Which of the following has become an enemy to the most important relationship of your life: work, sleep, TV, good books, music, exercise, hobbies, friends, family, church responsibilities, a clean house, or the garden? Take a look at your to-do list. Is communion with God number one on your list?

Faith

According to Oswald Chambers, "Faith never knows where it is being led, but it loves and knows the One Who is leading" (*My Utmost for His Highest,* p. 57).

"Faith is not intelligent understanding, faith is deliberate commitment to a Person where I see no way" (ibid., p. 63).

Fasting

"Fasting can bring breakthroughs in the spiritual realm that will never happen in any other way. It is a means of God's grace and blessing that should not be neglected any longer," states Richard J. Foster in his book *Celebration of Discipline.*

Fasting, when entered into for spiritual purposes, has the following benefits: it gives us clearer minds to commune with God; it helps us understand what controls us; it reminds us that we are sustained not by food, but by God; it helps us keep balance in our lives, weeding out the nonessentials; it increases our power in intercessory prayer and our concentration on spiritual things.

Goal

The goal of a prayer journey is to meet the King of Prayer Country. "Whenever the insistence is on the point that God answers prayer, we are off the track. The meaning of prayer is that we get hold of God, not of the answer" (*My Utmost for His Highest,* p. 27).

Holy Spirit

We must not only pray in Christ's name, but by the inspiration of the Holy Spirit. This explains what is meant when it is said that the Spirit "maketh intercession for us, with groanings which cannot be uttered. . . ." Such prayer God delights to answer. When with earnestness and intensity we breathe a prayer in the name of Christ, there is in that very intensity a pledge from God that He is about to answer our prayer "exceeding abundantly above all that we ask or think" (*Christ's Object Lessons,* p. 147).

Intercession

Prayers of intercession give God permission to work in another person's life. Our prayers for healing, salvation, or protection are unhindered by distance, political borders, or locked doors. We can surround loved ones thousands of miles away with the protection of holy angels through prayer. Our prayers can reach wherever God can reach.

A spirit of intercession will come among God's people before He comes. About this experience, Ellen White wrote: "Many were praising God. The sick were healed, and other miracles were wrought. A spirit of intercession was seen, even as was manifested before the great Day of Pentecost" (*Testimonies*, vol. 9, p. 126).

Joy

Joy is the currency used to pay for a vacation in Prayer Country. The psalmist reminds us to make a "sacrifice of thanksgiving." Ellen White suggests making daily "offerings of joy and gratitude . . . for the power of His grace" (*Testimonies*, vol. 5, p. 574).

Key

Prayer is the key to victorious Christian living.

> The darkness of the evil one encloses those who neglect to pray. The whispered temptations of the enemy entice them to sin; and it is all because they do not make use of the privileges that God has given them in the divine appointment of prayer. Why should the sons and daughters of God be reluctant to pray, when prayer is the key in the hand of faith to unlock heaven's storehouse, where are treasured the boundless resources of Omnipotence? (*Steps to Christ*, pp. 94, 95).

Levels

In her book *Prayer*, Beverly LaHaye lists five levels of communication with God.

Level 1: Prayer clichés. Using phrases such as "God bless our home" and "Lord, help me," or "Thank You for everything."

Level 2: Impersonal information. Describing a problem to God, bringing Him up to date with our needs.

Level 3: Giving our opinions and conclusions to God. Telling God what needs to be done about a problem and when

He needs to do it.

Level 4: Sharing our fears, dreams, and goals with God. Talking with God, as one friend to another, about those things that are important to us, trusting Him to act in our best interest.

Level 5: Praying intimately for others. Having such a deep relationship with God that He becomes a part of everything that we do or think. At this level, we share our unselfish concerns for others.

Listening

Prayer is conversing with God, a communication that goes both ways. There is giving as well as receiving, listening as well as talking.

"Be still, and know that I am God," He says in Psalm 46:10. It seems He is saying, "I've listened to you. Now be quiet and listen to Me. How can we be friends if you do all the talking? Don't you want to get to know Me?"

Mustard seed principle

Though the grain of mustard seed is so small, it contains that same mysterious life principle which produces growth in the loftiest tree. When the mustard seed is cast into the ground, the tiny germ lays hold of every element that God has provided for its nutriment, and it speedily develops a sturdy growth. If you have faith like this, you will lay hold upon God's word, and upon all the helpful agencies He has appointed. Thus your faith will strengthen, and will bring to your aid the power of heaven. The obstacles that are piled by Satan across your path, though apparently as insurmountable as the eternal hills, shall disappear before the demand of faith. "Nothing shall be impossible unto you" (*The Desire of Ages*, p. 431).

Necessity

Jesus Himself, while He dwelt among men, was often in prayer.... His humanity made prayer a necessity and a privilege. He found comfort and joy in communion with His Father. And if the Saviour of men, the Son of God, felt the need of prayer, how much more should feeble, sinful mortals feel the necessity of fervent, constant prayer (*Steps to Christ*, pp. 93, 94).

Obstructions

Without unceasing prayer and diligent watching we are in danger of growing careless and of deviating from the right path. The adversary seeks continually to obstruct the way to the mercy seat, that we may not by earnest supplication and faith obtain grace and power to resist temptation (*Steps to Christ,* p. 95).

What obstructions prevent you from praying?

Power

Prayer plugs you in to God's mighty power. "Power will come from God in answer to the prayer of faith" (*Gospel Workers,* p. 255).

In *Too Busy Not to Pray,* Hybels suggests that we read the Bible looking for the following: God's power over nature, God's power over circumstances, and God's power over people. List at least ten examples of God's power in each category. Such a study should convince you that God is indeed able to supply the power for any situation.

"Prayer moves the arm of Omnipotence" (*Christ's Object Lessons,* p. 172).

Perseverance

"Perseverance in prayer has been made a condition of receiving" (*Steps to Christ,* p. 97).

"If our trust in the Lord is real," George Mueller once said, "help will surely come." His life is an example of someone who persevered in prayer. He received thousands of answers to prayer, though for some he waited as long as twenty-nine years.

Could it be that some of your prayers have not yet been answered because you gave up too soon?

"For ye have need of patience, that after ye have done the will of God, ye might receive the promise" (Hebrews 10:36).

Quietness

> All who are under the training of God need the quiet hour for communion with their own hearts, with nature, and with God. In them is to be revealed a life that is not in harmony with the world, its customs, or its practices; and they need to have a personal experience in obtaining a knowledge of the will of God. We must individually hear Him speaking to the heart. When every other voice is hushed, and in quietness we wait before Him, the silence of the soul makes more distinct the voice of God (*The Ministry of Healing,* p. 58).

Reception

The Prayer of Reception is the label Coon puts on the process of claiming Bible promises with the ABC method: Ask, Believe, Claim. Ask for something God has already promised. Believe that God will keep His word. Claim or receive the promise by thanking God that you have the answer even before it is visible. You can know for sure that God will answer a Prayer of Reception because it claims something that God has promised.

A prayer asking for cleansing from sin is an example of a Prayer of Reception based on 1 John 1:9.

Relinquishment

The Prayer of Relinquishment is a prayer of submission to God's will. This is to be used when no direct promise applies. It is the prayer Christ prayed in Gethsemane: "Nevertheless not my will, but thine, be done." It is a prayer that turns over a situation to God and trusts Him to do what is best. It is a prayer that relinquishes our desire in the matter and yields unreservedly to God's will. We give God permission to do anything, regardless of the consequences.

A prayer for healing would need to be a Prayer of Relinquishment, since there is no specific promise to be claimed.

Solitude

Follow the example of Jesus, who "departed into a solitary place, and there prayed" (Mark 1:35).

Richard C. Foster suggests the following "steps to solitude":

1. Make use of little snatches of time during the day to spend a moment in silent prayer and meditation (example: waiting at a stop light, sleepless moments during the night).

2. Find a spot within your home that is your "quiet place" for prayer and meditation where no one is allowed to intrude.

3. On a quarterly basis, plan to withdraw from people for three or four hours to evaluate your goals and priorities.

4. Once a year, take a retreat to experience solitude, a time of listening only to God's voice.

Time

A journey to Prayer Country, like any other vacation trip, takes time. If it is an adventure we want badly enough, we will schedule the time to make it happen.

"In our private communions with God, time is essential to the value of the prayer. Much time spent with God is the secret of all successful praying," says E. M. Bounds in his book, *Power Through Prayer*. "God's acquaintance is not made hurriedly. He does not bestow His gifts on the casual or hasty comer and goer. To be much alone with God is the secret of knowing Him and of having influence with Him" (p. 43).

Five minutes of hurried prayer doesn't seem like much when compared to Martin Luther's two hours of planned prayer and Adoniram Judson's three hours of scheduled prayer time. How much time do you spend in prayer? Does prayer have a slot on your day's schedule of jobs to do?

Timing

God has reasons for the delays we experience in our prayer journey. Now is not always the best timing.

"Like the stars in the vast circuit of their appointed path, God's purposes know no haste and no delay" (*The Desire of Ages*, p. 32).

" 'My thoughts are not your thoughts, neither are your ways

my ways.' . . . 'As the heavens are higher than the earth, so are my ways higher than your ways and my thoughts than your thoughts' " (Isaiah 55:8, 9).

Unanswered prayer

In counseling individuals who are troubled because their prayers are unanswered, Bill Hybels uses the following outline:

If the request is wrong, God says, "No."
If the timing is wrong, God says, "Slow."
If you are wrong, God says, "Grow."

Victory

Victory in spiritual warfare comes on our knees. "There is need that many moments be spent in secret prayer, in close communion with God. Thus only can victories be won" (*Gospel Workers,* p. 365).

The darkness of the evil one encloses those who neglect to pray. The whispered temptations of the enemy entice them to sin; and it is all because they do not make use of the privileges that God has given them in the divine appointment of prayer (*Steps to Christ,* p. 95).

No man is safe for a day or an hour without prayer (*The Great Controversy,* p. 530).

Satan has come down in great power, knowing that his time is short. His angels are busy, and a great share of the people of God suffer themselves to be lulled to sleep by him. . . . I saw that it would be only by earnest effort and persevering prayer that this spell would be broken (*Testimonies,* vol. 1, p. 178).

Wishes

A wish is something hoped for, a desire for something not possessed. It is a far-off star that shows us where we'd like to go, but it has no power to get us there. The fulfillment of wishful thinking depends on chance and our own ability.

Prayer is a wish turned over to God, who has the power to make it happen. On our knees, we span the distance between hope and reality. Prayer depends on the almighty God, with whom all things are possible.

A journey to Prayer Country changes wishes into realities.

X-citing

An exciting adventure awaits you in the Great Land of Prayer!

You

YOU have been selected for an all-expense-paid tour of Prayer Country. Eleven tours await YOUR discovery!

Zacchaeus Principle, The

Zacchaeus went looking for Jesus, and he was not disappointed. He found a way to climb above the press of the crowd to see Jesus. So may we find a way to escape the pressures of our daily life through a journey into Prayer Country.

The Zacchaeus Principle: Those who enter Prayer Country seeking God will find Him.

For More Information

Tour One: The Palms Route

Foster, Richard J. *Celebration of Discipline*. San Francisco: Harper and Row, 1988.

Tour Two: The Eggs Expedition

Marshall, Catherine. *Adventures in Prayer*. New York: Ballantine Books, 1976.

____. "Adventures in Prayer." *Celebration!* January 1987.

Tour Three: The Promises Package

Coon, Glenn A. *The A, B, C's of Bible Prayer*. Kingsport, Tenn.: Kingsport Press, Inc., 1966.

____. *God's Promises Solve My Problems*. Mountain View, Calif.: Pacific Press, 1979.

____. *A Study Guide to the Prayer of Reception*. Kingsport, Tenn.: Kingsport Press, Inc., 1968.

____. *Youth Prays—God Answers*. Kingsport, Tenn.: Kingsport Press, Inc., 1968.

Shewmake, Carrol Johnson. *Practical Pointers to Personal Prayer*. Hagerstown, Md.: Review and Herald Publishing Association, 1989.

_____. *The Bible Promise Book.* Westwood, N.J.: Barbour and Company, Inc., 1985.

Tour Four: The ACTS Map

Hybels, Bill. *Too Busy Not to Pray.* Downers Grove, Ill.: Inter-Varsity Press, 1988.

Tour Five: The Text Tour

Jacobsen, Ruthie. "For a Beautiful Prayer Experience." *Oregon Conference Women's Ministries Newsletter,* vol. 3, no. 3, Summer 1989.

First Ladies Network. North American Division. vol. 1, no. 2, July 1989.

Tour Six: The List Cruise

Venden, Morris L. *The Answer Is Prayer.* Boise, Idaho: Pacific Press Publishing Association, 1988.

Tour Seven: The Sanctuary Safari

Andreasen, M. L. *The Sanctuary Service.* Hagerstown, Md.: Review and Herald Publishing Association, 1947.

Shcwmake, Carrol Johnson. *Practical Pointers to Personal Prayer.* Hagerstown, Md.: Review and Herald Publishing Association, 1989.

_____. *Sanctuary Secrets to Personal Prayer.* Hagerstown, Md.: Review and Herald Publishing Association, 1990.

Zarska, Carol. *A New and Living Way* (seven cassettes). American Cassette Ministries.

_____. *Knowing God in the Sanctuary* (four cassettes). American Cassette Ministries.

_____. *With Christ in the Sanctuary* (five cassettes). American Cassette Ministries.

_____. *The Final Conflict* (four cassettes). American Cassette Ministries.

Zarska, Carol, and Michael Curzon. *The Gospel and the Sanctuary* (ten cassettes). American Cassette Ministries.

_____. *Intercessory Prayer in the Sanctuary* (ten cassettes). American Cassette Ministries.

Tour Eight: The Bouquets Vacation

Richardson, Ione M. *Bouquets, With Love, Jesus.* Concerned Communications, 1989.

Tour Nine: The Journaling Trip

Broyles, Anne. *Journaling: A Spirit Journey.* Nashville, Tenn.: The Upper Room, 1988.

Hybels, Bill. *Too Busy Not to Pray.* Downers Grove, Ill.: Inter-Varsity Press, 1988.

Klug, Ronald. *How to Keep a Spiritual Journal.* Nashville: Thomas Nelson Publishers, 1982.

MacDonald, Gordon. *Ordering Your Private World.* Nashville: Oliver-Nelson, 1985.

Simons, George F. *Keeping Your Personal Journal.* New York: Ballantine Books, 1986.

Tour Ten: The PART PLAN

Hybels, Bill. *Too Busy Not to Pray.* Downers Grove, Ill.: Inter-Varsity Press, 1988.

MacDonald, Gordon. *Ordering Your Private World.* Nashville: Oliver-Nelson, 1985.

Ortlund, Anne. *The Disciplines of the Beautiful Woman*. Dallas: Word Books, 1984.

Tirabassi, Becky. *Releasing God's Power*. Nashville: Oliver-Nelson, 1990.

_____. *My Partner Prayer Notebook*. Nashville: Oliver-Nelson, 1990.

Tour Eleven: The TRIALS Trail

White, Ellen G. "The Call of Abraham." In *Patriarchs and Prophets*. Mountain View, Calif.: Pacific Press, 1958.

General Guides to Prayer Country

Andross, Matilda Erickson. *Alone With God*. Mountain View, Calif.: Pacific Press Publishing Association, 1929.

Bounds, E. M. *Power Through Prayer*. Springdale, Pa.: Whitaker House, 1983.

Bryant, David. *Concerts of Prayer*. Ventura, Calif.: Regal Books, 1988 (Group Tours).

Duewel, Wesley L. *Touch the World Through Prayer*. Grand Rapids, Mich.: Zondervan Publishing, 1986.

LaHaye, Beverly. *Prayer*. Nashville: Thomas Nelson Publishers, 1990.